HISTORY OF
THE ANCIENT AND MEDIEVAL WORLD

SECOND EDITION

VOLUME 1

THE FIRST CIVILIZATIONS

Marshall Cavendish
Reference
New York

Marshall Cavendish
99 White Plains Road
Tarrytown, New York 10591

www.marshallcavendish.us

Library of Congress Cataloging-in-Publication Data

History of the ancient and medieval world / [edited by Henk Dijkstra]. --
2nd ed.
        v. cm.
    Includes bibliographical references and index.
    Contents: v. 1. The first civilizations -- v. 2. Western Asia and the
Mediterranean -- v. 3. Ancient Greece -- v. 4. The Roman Empire -- v. 5. The
changing shape of Europe -- v. 6. The early Middle Ages in western Asia and
Europe -- v. 7. Southern and eastern Asia -- v. 8. Europe in the Middle Ages
-- v. 9. Western Asia, northern Europe, and Africa in the Middle Ages -- v.
10. The passing of the medieval world -- v. 11. Index.
    ISBN 978-0-7614-7789-1 (set) -- ISBN 978-0-7614-7791-4 (v. 1) -- ISBN
978-0-7614-7792-1 (v. 2) -- ISBN 978-0-7614-7793-8 (v. 3) -- ISBN
978-0-7614-7794-5 (v. 4) -- ISBN 978-0-7614-7795-2 (v. 5) -- ISBN
978-0-7614-7796-9 (v. 6) -- ISBN 978-0-7614-7797-6 (v. 7) -- ISBN
978-0-7614-7798-3 (v. 8) -- ISBN 978-0-7614-7799-0 (v. 9) -- ISBN
978-0-7614-7800-3 (v. 10) -- ISBN 978-0-7614-7801-0 (v. 11)
    1. History, Ancient. 2. Middle Ages. 3. Civilization, Medieval. I.
Dijkstra, Henk.
    D117.H57 2009
    940.1--dc22
                                                    2008060052

Printed in Malaysia

12 11 10 09 08 7 6 5 4 3 2 1

General Editor: Henk Dijkstra

Marshall Cavendish
Project Editor: Brian Kinsey
Publisher: Paul Bernabeo
Production Manager: Michael Esposito

Brown Reference Group
Project Editor: Chris King
Text Editors: Shona Grimbly, Charles Phillips
Designer: Lynne Lennon
Cartographers: Joan Curtis, Darren Awuah
Picture Researcher: Laila Torsun
Indexer: Christine Michaud
Managing Editor: Tim Cooke

PICTURE CREDITS

Cover: Wall painting from tomb of Ramses I in Valley of
the Kings, Egypt (Topham: Heaton).
Volume Contents: Sarcophagus in tomb of Tutankhamen
(Topham).

AKG Images: 8, 17, 21, 45, 48, 62, 113, 115, 125, Gerard
Degeorge 57, Electa 49, Herbert Kraft 23, Erich Lessing 9,
10, 11, 13, 14, 22, 35, 37, 38, 40, 43, 44, 47, 53, 63, 64, 90,
100, 114, 117, 120, 121, 122, 123, Nimtallah 95, Sambraus
20; **Shutterstock:** 83, CJ Photo 108, Philip Lange 29, Bill
McKelvie 93; **Topham:** 36, 58, 61, 67, 69, 105, 119, AA
World Travel Library 24, Alinari 27, Ann Ronan Picture
Library/HIP 15, AP 34, 93, British Museum/HIP 7, 55, 59,
74, 81, 84, 87, CM Dixon/HIP 39, 41, 51, Silvio Fiore 65,
116, 118, Christina Gascoigne 111, Doug Houton 30,
Charles Walker 12, 25, 26, 31, 85, 103, Dave Walsh 28;
Werner Forman: 16, 19, 33, 46, 50, 52, 60, 66, 68, 71, 75,
76, 77, 79, 82, 86, 88, 89, 91, 97, 98, 99, 102, 104, 106, 107,
109.

INTRODUCTION

Extensively revised to reflect the latest academic thinking, this updated edition of *History of the Ancient and Medieval World* traces the course of human history from the first development of stone tools by early hunter-gatherers to the spectacular artistic achievements of the Renaissance. In between, the set gives detailed accounts of the glories of the great civilizations of Egypt, Greece, and Rome, the rise of the Islamic world, and the growth of the early empires of the Americas. The period covered by the set saw many of the key cultural, political, and scientific developments in the history of humankind, from the development of writing and the invention of the wheel to the rise of the world's great religions and the evolution of the first democracies. The set thus offers the reader a fresh perspective on the historical events that shaped the modern world.

The text is accompanied by more than 1,000 illustrations and 50 full-color maps. Each chapter contains a separate time line, as well as boxed features that examine the lives of key historical figures, give expanded accounts of specific events, or look at major technological developments. Each 144-page volume features an index, a time line, and a glossary that are specific to that volume, as well as suggestions for further reading. In addition, the final volume of the set contains a comprehensive set index, a number of thematic indexes, and expanded glossary, time line, and further reading sections.

SET CONTENTS

VOLUME CONTENTS

EARLY HUMANS

The Stone Age, which lasted from around 2 million BCE until around 3500 BCE, saw several crucial breakthroughs in the development of human culture, the most important being the first use of stone tools and the advent of agriculture.

The earliest human beings lived on the grasslands of Africa around 2 million years ago. They were hunter-gatherers who survived on the wild plants, nuts, seeds, and berries they gathered and the meat of the small animals they hunted. Everything that is known about these people is based on the remains they left behind: their skeletons, the bones of the animals they ate, the materials they gathered and used, and, most of all, the tools they made.

The early humans made tools from a variety of materials (including wood, bone, antlers, and ivory), but mainly from stone. For that reason, this period of human development is called the Stone Age. It began when *Homo habilis* first made stone tools around 2 million BCE and lasted until the Bronze Age, which began around 3500 BCE in western Asia—before spreading to India around 3300 BCE, China around 3100 BCE, and northern Europe around 1900 BCE.

Types of tools

Historians divide the Stone Age into three periods, based on the type of stone tools being made. In the first part, called the Paleolithic period or Old Stone Age, people made tools from chipped stone. In the third part, called the Neolithic period or New Stone Age, they made tools from polished stone. In between came the Mesolithic or Middle Stone Age, when people were still making chipped-stone tools but were also beginning to make polished-stone tools.

In these three periods, there was also a gradual change in the basic way of life. In the Paleolithic period, humans lived as hunter-gatherers. In the Mesolithic period, people established seasonal camps, founded the first semipermanent settlements, and took tentative steps toward farming by beginning to harvest wild crops and domesticate animals. Then, in the Neolithic period, people established the first farming settlements, where they planted and harvested crops and raised animals for food.

Tools in the Old Stone Age

Toolmakers in the Paleolithic period used one piece of stone to chip away at another, thereby creating a sharp edge on the second stone. They worked with quartz or quartzite, but when they could, they used flint and obsidian, which were easier to chip. For more than a million years, a stone tool called the hand-ax was made by stoneworkers in Africa and Europe. People used these hand-axes to chop plants, to cut and shape wood and bone, and to chop meat.

By around 35,000 BCE, people were also making carefully shaped stone knives and spearheads. They were also fashioning fish-hooks and harpoons from bone and antler, as well as bows and arrows and wooden spear-throwers. The spear-thrower, which functioned as an extension of the human arm, resembled a long wooden bat, grooved to hold the handle of the spear. Using this tool, a man could throw a spear over a much greater distance and with much greater force. By this stage, humans were relying more and more on hunting to provide food.

An eye for beauty

Some of the Stone Age tools were beautifully made and decorated. Several hand-axes fashioned in this period were painstakingly worked to a symmetrical shape, and the spear-throwers often had artistic decorations. Around 30,000 BCE, people made the first of the remarkable cave paintings that survive from this period (see box, page 11).

The people of the Stone Age also carved statuettes. One example is the Venus of Willendorf, which was found in Austria. A limestone figure of a naked woman measuring approximately 4 inches (10 cm) in height, the Venus was carved around 24,000 BCE and is believed to be one of the world's oldest works of art. Historians think the figurine probably depicted a fertility goddess. Another example of prehistoric art is an ivory head just 1.5 inches (3.5 cm) in height. Found at Brassempouy, near Landes in France, the head was carved around 20,000 BCE. Known as the Venus of Brassempouy, it has well-defined features that look as if they were carved from life. It is probably the world's earliest known human portrait.

The end of the ice ages

The Paleolithic era occurred during the most recent in a long series of ice ages. This ice age—which is called the Pleistocene period by geologists—lasted from around 1.6 million years ago until around 10,000 BCE. Several previous ice ages had occurred, the earliest beginning around 570 million years ago. For parts of the Pleistocene period, most of Europe, Asia, and North America was covered by great sheets of ice. During these times, the ancestors of modern humans lived mainly in regions close to the equator. In these periods, sea levels were as much as 450 feet (137 m) lower

This hand-ax, made around 400,000 BCE, was found in Suffolk, England. Hand-axes were used for a wide variety of purposes.

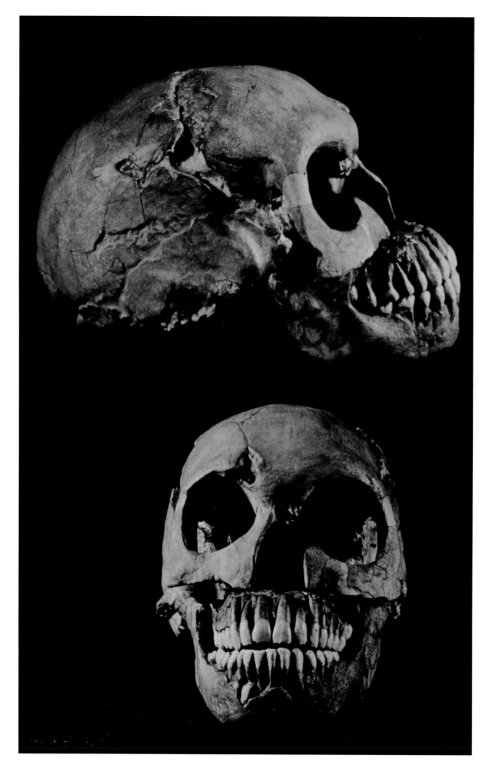

period an ice age came every 100,000 years. In between these extremes were milder periods called interglacials.

Changes afoot

The very beginning of the Mesolithic period in Europe coincided with the end of the last ice age around 10,000 BCE. As the ice retreated in the Northern Hemisphere, the climate became warmer and wetter. As the ice caps melted, ocean levels rose and new lakes were created. Tundra landscape—mostly covered in grass and moss with a few birch and willow trees—gradually retreated northward. The reindeer that thrived in the tundra conditions also went northward. Further south, forests grew, first consisting of pine and hazel and then—as the climate grew warmer still—oak and spruce.

These changes meant that the people of the Mesolithic era had to adapt to survive. In particular, they developed more sophisticated hunting skills. Where they had previously been able to follow large migrating herds of bison, reindeer, and mammoth, they now tracked small groups and single animals through trees. They learned to hunt roe and red deer,

than they currently are. At other times, the ice retreated northward, and great forests grew on the land that was uncovered. As a result, people moved north. By studying seabed deposits, geologists have discovered that in the Pleistocene

boars, wild pigs, and wild ox in the forests, in the open fields, and in the river deltas. People began to kill and eat birds as hunters became more skilled in the use of bows and arrows. They also probably learned to use snares and traps, although no remains of these items have been found to provide proof.

Mesolithic people also began to hunt in the company of dogs. The first domesticated dogs were probably the cubs of slaughtered wolves. If the hunters gave the cubs food and allowed them to play around the campfire, the cubs would have been rejected by their own wild packs. The cubs would then have become dependent on humans.

In some areas, people discovered the pleasures of eating fish and waterfowl. They used bone hooks and harpoons to fish in rivers, lakes, and oceans. Using canoes, they also hunted seals, porpoises, and small whales. They gathered and ate shellfish. Mesolithic craftsmen began to mount tools on handles. One common Mesolithic tool, called the microlith, was a small sharp piece of stone. Several

The Venus of Willendorf, created around 24,000 BCE, is one of the earliest human works of art.

THE RISE OF MODERN HUMANS

Humans and the great apes descend from a common ancestor that lived around 10 to 8 million years ago and walked on four legs. By around 4 million years ago an ancestor of humans called *Australopithecus* (southern ape) was living in Africa. *Australopithecus* walked on two legs but had a much smaller brain than present-day humans. A later ancestor called *Homo habilis* (skilled man) developed around 2 million years ago and was the first to make and use tools. *Homo habilis* was also the first human ancestor to leave Africa, doing so around 1 million to 400,000 years ago. These humans were able to build shelters and light fires to cope with the colder conditions in Europe.

Homo sapiens (thinking man) developed around 1 million years ago. As their name suggests, these humans had much larger brains than their ancestors. The first modern humans—or *Homo sapiens sapiens*—developed in Africa around 100,000 BCE. For tens of thousands of years, these people lived alongside another human subspecies, *Homo sapiens neanderthalensis* or Neanderthal man, gradually spreading out around the world. Modern humans were living in western Asia by 100,000 BCE, in Europe by 50,000 BCE, and in the Americas and Australia by 30,000 BCE. By around 30,000 BCE, modern humans had replaced the Neanderthals completely.

some regions and at some times of the year, they lived—like their ancestors before them—in caves.

The first boats

Simple canoes built by Mesolithic fishermen are the first known boats. The world's oldest known boat is a dugout canoe, made from a tree trunk, that was found at Pesse in the Netherlands and dates to 6200 BCE. The canoe's maker was a member of a group of people who lived throughout the regions adjacent to the North Sea and the Black Sea. From the remains they left behind, it is known that they lived primarily by hunting and had several specialized tools made of bone, antler, and stone. They set up camps in dry, elevated spots near fresh water and lived in wooden frame huts covered with straw. They supplemented their diet in different ways, according to the season: in the spring, they fished for salmon, while in the summer and autumn, they gathered wild fruits and hazelnuts from the forests. They also collected eggs and the edible parts of water plants. So much is known about these people because some of their remains survived in peat bogs, which preserve otherwise perishable materials such as wood and bone.

The first permanent settlements

From the remains they discover, archaeologists are able to identify groups of people who shared a way of life and used the same kinds of tools as one another. A cohesive group of this type is known as a culture. In western Asia, the peoples of the Natufian culture were forerunners of the first farmers. Living in Palestine and southern Syria between around 10,000 and 9000 BCE, they gradually spread out along the entire eastern coast of the Mediterranean Sea. They

The Venus of Brassempouy, carved around 20,000 BCE, is one of the earliest sculptures to depict human facial features.

microliths were mounted together on a shaft and used for spearing fish. Archaeologists often find microliths alongside a variety of bone, antler, and wooden tools in remains from the Mesolithic period.

The Mesolithic people lived in temporary camps in established hunting areas and founded semipermanent seasonal settlements in other regions. In

lived by fishing, hunting gazelles, and harvesting wild grasses. They developed the world's first mowing tools—straight-handled bone sickles set with flint blades to cut the wild grasses—and used stone mortars and pestles for grinding the grain.

These people almost certainly did not cultivate grain themselves; they merely gathered grasses that grew unattended in the wild. They also did not raise any domesticated animals for consumption. However, they took the first significant steps from a nomadic hunter-gatherer lifestyle to a settled agricultural way of life. The Natufians were ahead of their time in that they established permanent settlements. They used cemeteries to bury their dead and placed personal items, including stone artworks and bones with decorative carvings, in the burial places alongside the bodies.

While some Natufian people lived in caves, others lived in villages. It was Natufians who established the original settlement at Jericho in the valley of the Jordan River, where some of the first cultivated wheat and barley has been found (see box, page 13).

CAVE ART IN THE STONE AGE

Around 30,000 BCE, the world's first known artists emerged when people of the Old Stone Age began to paint on cave walls. The artists created remarkably life-like images of the large animals they hunted—bison, reindeer, mammoths, horses, and a form of wild ox called the auroch. The people drew directly on the rock using lumps of charcoal and earth pigments to produce images in black, brown, yellow, and red; in some places, they ground the pigments, mixed them with water, and applied them to the walls by brushing or blowing. The images were often in inaccessible and dark parts of the caves and were probably religious shrines.

The best examples of cave paintings are those created by the Solutrean and Magdalenian peoples in northern Spain and southern France between around 16,000 and 8000 BCE. The dramatic animal scenes in the cave at Lascaux, near Montignac in the Dordogne, France, were painted around 14,000 BCE and may have been intended to bring power to hunters.

These stone tools date to between 50,000 and 10,000 BCE. They were probably used as scrapers.

This Stone Age painting of a bison is found in a cave near Lascaux, France. The paintings at Lascaux are among the best preserved examples of cave art.

The first farmers

The inhabitants of a village at Abu Hureyra, on the Euphrates River in northern Syria, are often identified as the world's first farmers. The oldest remains there, from around 1100 BCE, were left by hunter-gatherers who hunted gazelles and gathered wild barley, rye, and lentils. However, a second wave of residents, who lived permanently in the village from around 8500 BCE onward, grew a domesticated form of barley, oats, chick-peas, and lentils. They used mortars and pestles to dehusk the grains and large grinding stones to process them. This work, which would have taken several hours, was done daily, because the seeds did not keep once dehusked.

The development of farming in the Near East and Europe marks the end of

JERICHO

Jericho, on the west side of the valley of the Jordan River and now in the West Bank, Palestine, is one of the world's oldest continuous settlements, dating back to around 9000 BCE. Jericho is mentioned several times in the Bible. It is chiefly famous as the first town attacked by the Israelites after they crossed the Jordan River (probably in the 13th century BCE). It was later the site of one of Herod the Great's residences, where he died in 4 BCE.

The oldest remains of Jericho are at Tell es-Sultan, around 1 mile (1.6 km) north of the Roman and New Testament city. The word *tell* is Arabic meaning "mound," and refers to the small hill, several feet tall, built up over thousands of years by succeeding waves of inhabitants, each building on top of its predecessors' remains.

The people of the Natufian culture were the first to establish a permanent settlement at Jericho.

Between around 8350 and 7370 BCE, they established a walled settlement—large enough to contain 2,000 to 3,000 people—with round houses of sun-hardened clay tiles. There was a defensive tower in the center of one of the walls. The city's inhabitants grew emmer wheat, barley, and pulses; they also raised domesticated goats for food. Between 7220 and 5850 BCE, a new settlement was established with square mud-brick houses raised on stone foundations.

Subsequently, generation after generation left their mark on Jericho. The remains of New Testament Jericho include an exceptional façade believed to have been part of Herod's palace. A third settlement nearby, the Jericho of the Crusader era (1095–1291 CE), formed the basis of the modern city.

These walls provided protection to the town of Jericho and date back to the earliest period of its history.

the Mesolithic period and the beginning of the Neolithic period. Gradually—in what historians call the Neolithic Revolution—farming became established in the Fertile Crescent, which runs from the Mediterranean coast of present-day Turkey, Syria, Israel, and Jordan through Iraq and Iran to the Persian Gulf.

The agricultural way of life then spread out from this area to southern Russia, India, and northern Africa—and to Europe. The spread was a very gradual development that took thousands of years. The Neolithic period that began in western Asia around 9000 BCE did not really start in northern Europe until around 4000 to 3000 BCE, when farming became established there. The Mesolithic period was thus relatively short in western Asia, where it lasted for around 1,000 years (from around 10,000 to 9000 BCE), but much longer in northern Europe, where it lasted for around 6,000 years (from around 10,000 to 4000 BCE or even later).

Independently from these developments in the Fertile Crescent, people in other parts of the world were also turning from hunting and gathering to farming. In Peru, early farmers cultivated edible gourds and potatoes around 8000 BCE and beans by 7000 BCE. In China and southeast Asia, people began to domesticate pigs (c. 7000 BCE) and chickens (c. 6000 BCE) and to cultivate millet (c. 6000 BCE) and rice (c. 5000 BCE). In Mesoamerica, which is roughly the area now called Central America, people were cultivating maize by around 6000 to 5500 BCE.

The spread of farming

The agricultural way of life spread across the land bridge of Turkey to Europe and across the Aegean Sea to Greece. A permanent farming settlement at Çatalhüyük in present-day Turkey has been dated to around 6700 to 5650 BCE. Its people cultivated grains, nuts, and seeds and raised animals for food. They lived in rectangular mudbrick houses, which were fitted with platforms for working, sitting, and sleeping and included ovens and hearths. The houses were built together in a large block, and their interior walls were decorated with paintings and reliefs, usually figures of

A wheat field in Galilee, Israel. The region was one of the first areas of the world to be farmed by humans.

animals and geometric patterns. The people worshipped a fertility goddess and the bull.

Another Neolithic farming settlement in the area was located at Çayönü, also in present-day Turkey. The remains unearthed there include what are probably the world's oldest containers, made from hollowed-out stones, as well as agricultural tools, including scythes and millstones that were used to process grain.

Around this time (before 6000 BCE), the first farming settlements in Europe were established on the island of Crete and on the plain of Thessaly in Greece. The farming revolution had spread along sea routes established by fishermen. At sites such as Knossos on Crete and Argissa-Magoula in Greece, people grew a domesticated form of barley and began to develop trading links with other settlements.

Trade and population growth

Farming proved a more efficient way to find food than hunting and gathering, and the first farmers discovered they were able to build up food surpluses. People had leisure time to turn to crafts and made the first earthenware containers. They were also able to trade with other settlements. The farming settlement at Çatalhüyük was the center of trade in obsidian, a type of natural glass.

The new agricultural way of life was spread along the often very extensive trading networks. In addition, the efficiency of farming led to an unparalleled population explosion, which resulted in the forced migration of groups and families. Seeking new land, they carried the farming lifestyle with them. However, the migrants were also influenced by the way of life they discovered. The end result was a high degree of variety among farming cultures.

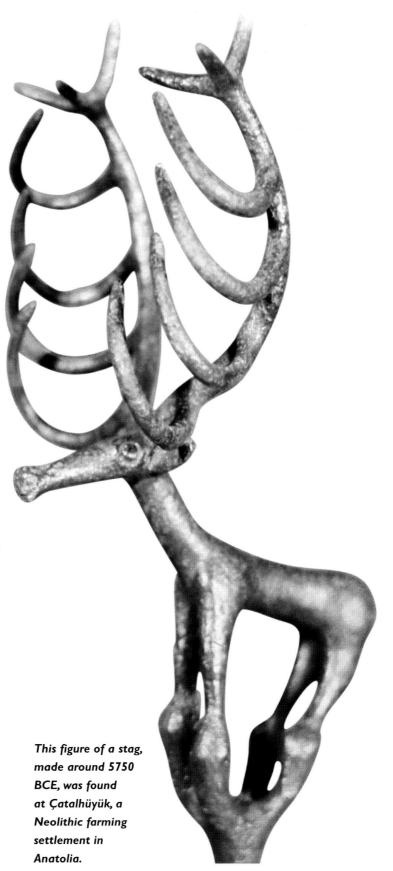

This figure of a stag, made around 5750 BCE, was found at Çatalhüyük, a Neolithic farming settlement in Anatolia.

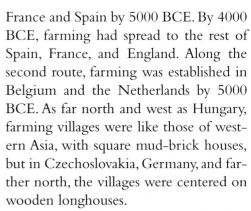

These clay pots were made by the people of the Bükk culture of northeastern Hungary.

The early farmers knew nothing of fertilization or crop rotation. They repeatedly planted crops on the same plots of land. This led to depletion of the soil and ever-decreasing yields for the farmers. It is no coincidence that the most successful early agricultural civilizations were those in Egypt and Mesopotamia, where the rivers flooded each year and kept the fields fertile.

Farmers in less hospitable lands further north regularly had to find new land. They often burned off a section of forest in order to plant the land, a process known as "slash and burn farming." Sometimes, years after leaving a place, they would return to an area only to find it occupied by other people, which could lead either to conflict or to compromise and assimilation.

The earthenware trail

Broadly speaking, farming spread east to west across Europe via two routes: first, along the coast of the Mediterranean Sea, and second, along the corridor of the Vardar, Danube, and Rhine rivers. Along the first route, farming had reached the Italian Peninsula, the island of Sicily, and the Mediterranean coasts of France and Spain by 5000 BCE. By 4000 BCE, farming had spread to the rest of Spain, France, and England. Along the second route, farming was established in Belgium and the Netherlands by 5000 BCE. As far north and west as Hungary, farming villages were like those of western Asia, with square mud-brick houses, but in Czechoslovakia, Germany, and farther north, the villages were centered on wooden longhouses.

The Neolithic farmers were the first to make earthenware pots; their predecessors probably used wooden pots that have left no remains. Archaeologists can trace the movement of Neolithic farmer-settlers by the remains of their earthenware pots. In the more northerly parts of Europe, for example, the important Linearbandkeramik culture is named after pots with a characteristic decorative pattern of wavy or zigzag lines. The Linearbandkeramik culture spread along the valleys of the Rhine, Dniester, Weichsel, and Elbe rivers and became established in Poland, Germany, the Netherlands, Belgium, France, and

Switzerland, while also branching off toward the Baltic coast.

East and west

The Linearbandkeramik farming communities were established in the Low Countries along the North Sea coasts by 5000 BCE. The settlers chose areas with loessial soil (a fine-grained, yellowish brown soil) because of its fertility and because the areas where it was found were high and dry enough for farming. The farmers broke the ground with sticks, stone axes, and rocks. They grew barley and three types of wheat (emmer, einkorn, and durum), while raising cattle, sheep, goats, and pigs in fenced-off areas. Some of the villages were quite large, containing dozens of houses. Living mainly on higher ground, the people had limited contact with groups that still followed the old Mesolithic way of life in the river valleys.

A settlement of Linearbandkeramik culture that was excavated at Sittard in the Netherlands consisted of no fewer than 44 farms. Most of the houses were more than 30 yards (27.43 m) long and around 7 yards (6.4 m) wide. The northwest parts of the buildings were more solidly built and were probably used as living quarters, while the other parts of the buildings were sheds or stalls for the animals.

Archaeologists make a distinction between the Western Linear Pottery culture, which existed in northwestern Europe, and similar cultures that existed to the east. One example of Eastern Linear Pottery culture is the Bükk culture that flourished in the mountains of northeastern Hungary. The Bükk people are famous for the sophisticated nature of their pottery, which was more delicate than that produced in the west and was decorated with more complex patterns.

See also:

The Age of the Megaliths (volume 1, page 18)

This prehistoric axhead, made out of an elk's antler, was found in present-day Germany.

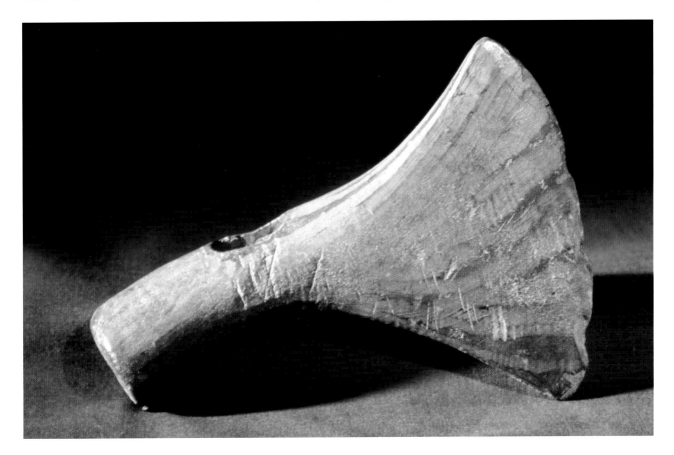

THE AGE OF THE MEGALITHS

In northern and western Europe, the Neolithic period or New Stone Age lasted for around 3,000 years. During this time, a number of impressive stone monuments were built, including the arrangements of stones at Carnac, Stonehenge, and Avebury.

Around 5000 BCE, people in central and northern Europe began to settle in farming villages, abandoning a seminomadic lifestyle to live by raising crops and keeping animals. This change marked the end of the Mesolithic period (or Middle Stone Age) and the beginning of the Neolithic period (or New Stone Age) in this area.

In the so-called Fertile Crescent of the Middle East, the Neolithic period began much earlier. There, the first farming villages had been established between around 8500 and 8000 BCE. The Neolithic farming revolution had spread slowly westward and northward over thousands of years. In central-northern Europe, the peoples of the Linearbandkeramik, Rössen, and Michelsberg cultures were among the first settled farmers.

Rössen and Michelsberg

The Rössen and Michelsberg cultures were successors to the Linearbandkeramik culture, which flourished between around 5000 and 4500 BCE. The Rössen peoples thrived between around 4500 and 3500 BCE in western Germany, parts of northern France, the southeastern Low Countries, and the Rhineland region. The Michelsberg peoples lived along the Rhine River, in Belgium, and in the Paris basin between around 4400 and 3500 BCE. They are sometimes seen as a late subgroup of the Rössen peoples but are more often viewed as their successors. The cultures take their names from excavated sites in Germany.

In settlements of the Rössen culture, people lived in longhouses like those used by the Linearbandkeramik settlers before them. Some of the houses were 165 feet (50 m) long, and the villages included defensive stockades and towers. The people buried their dead in cemeteries adjacent to the village. Michelsberg groups also lived in large houses, usually in hilltop settlements defended by palisades and wide ditches. Both groups clearly needed to defend themselves against raiders or rival farming clans who were looking for land.

Both the Rössen and Michelsberg groups were accomplished potters. While the Rössen peoples made highly decorated ceramics, Michelsberg artisans produced mostly undecorated tulip beaker pottery (so-called because the slender beakers were shaped like a tulip flower). The settlements of both peoples were associated with mining and trading in flint (see box, page 23).

The funnel-beaker culture

Between around 4000 and 2500 BCE, a new culture arose in large parts of

This pot was made by the bell-beaker people who lived in central and western Europe. The culture takes its name from the distinctive shape of their pottery.

central-northern Europe. Archaeologists call it the funnel-beaker culture because its people made conical earthenware beakers with funnel-shaped rims. The funnel-beaker people covered a wide area. They lived in north, central, and east Germany, in Poland, in eastern parts of the Netherlands, and farther north in southern Scandinavia—in Denmark, southern Sweden, and southern Norway. They also lived in the Czech Republic, northern Slovakia, northern Austria, and western Ukraine.

The funnel-beaker people were farmers who supplemented their food supply by hunting. They grew barley and wheat and raised cows, sheep, goats, and pigs. They usually kept their animals penned within fenced areas, feeding them largely on elm leaves. The funnel-beaker people used "slash and burn" methods; they cleared plots for growing crops by burning down trees, and when the soil became depleted, they cleared another adjacent plot, leaving the depleted one as meadowland. They also hunted beaver, otter, red deer, roe deer, and wild boar and fished for pike and bass. They mined flint both for their own use and to trade with other areas—for example, parts of Scandinavia—where the rock was not found.

The villages that the funnel-beaker people lived in were often large, as were the houses within them. In Jutland (roughly present-day Denmark), archaeologists have excavated a vast building raised by funnel-beaker people on heavy beams driven into the ground. It was more than 250 feet (76 m) long and contained 26 rooms. Several family groups must have lived in this single building. This settlement may not have been typical, however. In Oldenburg, Germany, a funnel-beaker village had 40 separate houses, each either 13 feet by 16 feet or 16 feet by 22 feet (3.7 m by 4.8 m or 4.8 m by 6.7 m). All had two rooms and a porch. The walls were made of woven fibres and plastered with clay. The floors were made of tree trunks.

The funnel-beaker people usually built their villages near areas that were rich in peat. In the peat bogs close to their settlements, they made offerings of bone picks, tool handles, bowls, and wooden paddles to the gods or ancestors. Archaeologists have even found an earthenware pot containing a meal of eggs, fish, and two types of meat. The offerings they left have survived because peat bogs tend to preserve objects that would disintegrate in ordinary soil.

These stones form part of the stone circle at Avebury, England. Two other important Neolithic sites, the West Kennet Long Barrow and Silbury Hill, are found nearby.

The funnel-beaker people were skilled potters. As well as the funnel beakers that give the culture its name, they made collared bottles, spherical bottles with a protruding edge at the top, suitable for fastening to a carrying cord. They also made pitchers, bowls, platters, and baking sheets—large tiles of fired clay used to hold food for baking. Although the funnel-beaker people spread out over a large geographical area, all their pottery had a similar style and decorative pattern. Before firing, the clay was marked with a wooden or bone spatula. Some pieces were decorated with a stick wrapped in a thread.

Farming tools

The first farmers in central and northern Europe used digging sticks as tools. The farmers were often turning soil in cleared land that was still thick with tree stumps. Later, they developed a primitive plow, called an ard. This tool dug a single furrow but did not turn over soil as a conventional plow does. At first, farmers dragged plows by hand, but they soon began to pull them with cattle and oxen. The funnel-beaker people were the first Europeans to use draft oxen.

At the same time that the funnel-beaker people were flourishing in central Europe, settlers in Somerset, southern England, were building a wooden trackway across the swampy region between the Mendips and the Quantock Hills. They cut lengths of lime, oak, and ash trees and built them into a narrow footpath that ran for around 1.5 miles (almost 2 km). The footway was supported by a V-shape made from crossed lengths of wood that were pegged together and driven into heavy poles secured underwater. Very precise tree-ring dating has established that the pathway was built in the spring of 3806 BCE and that the surviving path lay on top of an earlier one that was made around 3838 BCE.

At around this time, people also developed a primitive sled. Hauling these sleds became easier when people thought to put lengths of tree trunks beneath them. It may be that the wheel was invented as a result of this innovation. Wheeled carts were being used in

This burial was made by people of the Rössen culture. The grave was found in Germany.

THE BRONOCICE POT

One of the pots made by craftsmen of the funnel-beaker culture was marked with what may be the world's earliest depiction of a wheeled vehicle. Made around 3500 BCE, it is named the Bronocice pot, after its finding place of Bronocice in Poland.

The image scratched on the pot resembles a four-wheeled wagon. It suggests that vehicles pulled by cattle may have been in use by people of the funnel-beaker culture in the middle of the fourth millennium BCE. This date is several hundred years earlier than the date usually given for the first use of wheeled vehicles in Mesopotamia. The discovery of the pot has thus led historians to question traditional ideas about the wheel's invention.

Mesopotamia and the Caucasus by around 3250 BCE, but an illustration on the Bronocice pot—found in Poland by archaeologists in 1976 CE—suggests that they may have been used in central Europe even earlier.

Tombs of earth and stone

The funnel-beaker people buried their dead in large *tumuli* (mounds). The corpse was usually laid to rest in a sleeping position, lying on his or her side, with one arm up toward the head and the knees drawn up. A mound of earth, usually oval, was piled over the body.

The graves within the burial mounds were often contained within stone chambers; sometimes, in the case of large burial grounds, they were approached by a long passage. Some of the funnel-beaker *tumuli* were used as communal graves, in which the people buried their dead, generation after generation.

This dolmen is located near Evora, Portugal. Dolmens originally served as burial chambers and were covered in earth.

FLINT MINING

Flint is a very hard form of granular quartz, usually brown or gray in color. Early humans found flint to be one of the best materials for making tools and weapons. For many millennia, people had gathered flint where they found it in isolated outcroppings. Then, around 30,000 BCE, people began to mine flint from seams on the earth's surface. Later, sometime between 5000 and 4000 BCE, people began to hack out deeper mines for flint.

Archaeologists have examined flint mines from this period at Spiennes, Belgium, and discovered how these miners worked. First, they dug out surface layers, and then, they hacked out vertical shafts, some up to 50 feet (15 m) deep. When they came to a layer of flint, they constructed horizontal tunnels radiating outward from the point of discovery. They used pickaxes with blades of deer antler or flint fitted onto wooden handles.

Work in the mines was dirty and dangerous. Miners worked in tunnels less than 3 feet (1 m) high, with a little lighting provided by chalk lamps and in the midst of clouds of dust or gravel. The miners hacked the flint deposits out of the chalk in which they were found and then carried the lumps of flint to the surface while dumping the chalk pieces in abandoned mine tunnels. They occasionally tried to support the roof of the mine with strong sapling poles, but cave-ins were a constant threat. In a mine at Obourg, Belgium, archaeologists discovered the skeleton of a miner still clutching his pickax, clearly buried by a sudden roof-collapse as he worked. The flint lumps the miners carried to the surface were roughly processed in workshops near the mine and then traded in that unfinished condition.

The two flint daggers shown here were made between 2000 and 1700 BCE and found in Denmark. Flint was a valuable commodity in the Neolithic period.

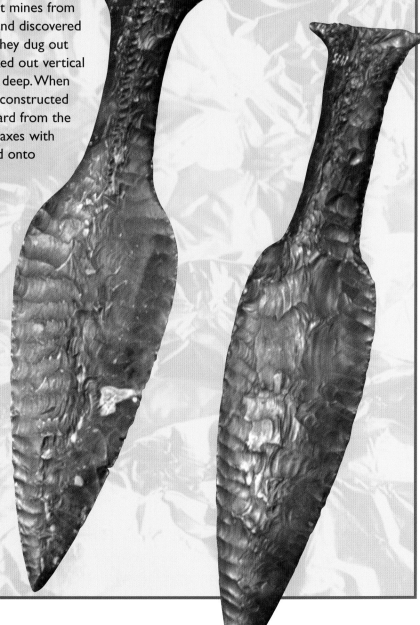

The Grand Menhir at Locmariaquer, France, is the largest standing stone known to have existed. It now lies broken into four separate pieces.

The dead were buried with offerings including tools, weapons, and stone and later bronze pots and pans filled with food and drink. Death was apparently regarded as a transition into further life, and the person who died was expected to require tools and other everyday items in his or her new existence.

Neolithic megaliths

Burial mounds were often marked by circles of poles, circular trenches, or stone monuments. They are one example of a great range of stone monuments left by the funnel-beaker people and their contemporaries and successors in Neolithic Europe. Many of the monuments featured great slabs of stone known as megaliths—from the ancient Greek words *megas*, meaning "great," and *lithos*, meaning "stone."

One common arrangement of megaliths is the dolmen. The dolmen grave consisted of a stone chamber built from two or more vertical stones supporting a vast horizontal slab. Many of these graves, which look a little like a great stone table, have been found in Brittany (western France), and the name *dolmen* derives from the words for "stone table" in the local language, Breton. The vast stones, which formed the inner chamber of a burial mound, were originally covered with earth, but at most archaeological sites, the earth has been dug away to reveal the stones.

In addition to Brittany, Neolithic dolmens were built in Portugal, Spain, and the Netherlands, as well as in the British Isles, where there are several in Wales, Cornwall, and Ireland. One celebrated example of a smaller dolmen is the Poulnabrone dolmen in the Burren, County Clare, Ireland. Built between around 3800 and 3200 BCE, it consists of a horizontal capstone measuring 12 feet by 7 feet (3.6 m by 2.1 m) supported by two vertical megaliths, each measuring 6 feet (2 m). Within the dolmen chamber, archaeologists found the bones of 16 adults, 6 young people, and a baby, with grave goods including a bone pendant, a polished stone axe, several flint arrowheads, and two quartz crystals.

Some dolmens were built on a very large scale. Probably the largest of all is the Dolmen of Menga in Andalucia, Spain, which contains 32 megaliths—including one that weighs 200 tons (180 metric tons). The dolmen chamber is 13 feet (4 m) tall and 80 feet (25 m) across and was probably used for years as a burial place for local rulers. When archaeologists excavated the site, they found hundreds of skeletons.

Some tombs were laid out with a long, low approach passage and are known as passage tombs. One remarkable example is found at Newgrange, County Meath, Ireland. Built between around 3300 and 2900 BCE, this great burial mound contains a passage that is almost 60 feet (18 m) long and leads into a burial chamber that is 20 feet (6 m) tall. The burial chamber is cruciform (cross-shaped) and contained a number of stone containers into which the cremated remains of local leaders were placed. Most remarkable of all, the passage was aligned very precisely so that the rising sun shines down it on the morning of the winter solstice. The sun shines through a special hole, which archaeologists call a roofbox, just above the entrance. Standing by the entrance is a great stone slab carved with a triple spiral decoration.

Standing stones and alignments

Neolithic masons also raised vast standing stones called menhirs. These are found either singly or in circles, ellipses,

This stone passage leads into the heart of the tomb at Newgrange.

or long rows called alignments, which probably had a religious or processional purpose. Archaeologists do not know whether any of the menhirs were originally associated with graves.

Menhirs were constructed most commonly in western Europe, particularly in Brittany. The name is derived from the Breton words *men*, meaning "stone," and *hir*, meaning "long." However, menhirs are also found in Romania and Scandinavia. The menhir at Locmariaquer in Brittany is the largest known to have existed. It once stood around 65 feet (22 m) tall. However, it was toppled by an earthquake in 1722 and today lies in four broken pieces on the ground. When whole, it was up to 13 feet (4 m) thick; overall, it weighed more than 380 tons (345 metric tons). Some experts believe it was part of the alignment of menhirs at Carnac, which lies around 7 miles (12 km) away.

More than 3,000 menhirs are arranged in alignments at Carnac. Some were raised as early as 4500 BCE, but most date to around 3400 BCE. There are three major groups of alignments, with the main example, Menec, consist-

ing of 11 rows that converge over more than 3,800 feet (1,160 m), running west to east. Some historians suggest that the remains of stone circles can be seen at either end of this alignment. The alignments at Carnac were probably used as a ceremonial walkway, although there is some evidence that they were laid out in accordance with the position of the sun at various key seasonal dates, suggesting that they may have been part of a vast solar or astronomical temple.

Stone circles

In southern England, there are two much more complete examples of the stone circles that historians believe once stood at the ends of the Menec alignment at Carnac. The most celebrated is at Stonehenge near Salisbury in Wiltshire (see box, page 29). It was first established in the late fourth millennium BCE, at the beginning of the Bronze Age, but its main features were constructed a good deal later, not before around 2100 BCE. Just under 20 miles (30 km) north of Stonehenge stands another circle at Avebury, also in Wiltshire. This circle was in position by around 2500 BCE. It con-

The burial mound at Newgrange in Ireland is one of the best preserved examples of a Neolithic passage tomb.

sists of 27 sandstone pillars, each weighing up to 45 tons (40 metric tons), standing in a circle 1,000 feet (305 m) across within an outer circle formed by a chalk bank 1,400 feet (425 m) across and 20 feet (6 m) high. Within the bank is a circular ditch that was originally 30 feet (9 m) deep. Some of the stones that are still standing in this circle are 19 feet (6 m) tall; smaller ones are 8 feet (2.5 m) tall. There are also the remains of two smaller stone circles within the circumference of the larger one.

The outer chalk circle at Avebury has four entrances. Archaeologists have uncovered evidence of an avenue that was 50 feet (15 m) wide and ran 1 mile (1.6 km) from the eastern entrance to a wooden temple (the Sanctuary) on Overton Hill. This processional way, which the archaeologists call Kennet Way, was marked out by pairs of standing stones facing each other across the avenue.

Earth mounds

The large circle at Avebury dates from around 2500 BCE, while its smaller inner circles are perhaps 100 years older. However, religious rituals were being performed in the area at the nearby West Kennet Long Barrow as early as 3700 BCE. The Long Barrow, a burial mound that is 320 feet long and 8 feet high (98 m by 2.5 m), is oriented on an east-west axis. It is a fine example of a Neolithic passage grave; five burial chambers

These giant stones, or menhirs, are just a few of the 3,000 such stones that are found at Carnac, France, and make up the largest collection in the world.

27

These standing stones are found near the West Kennet Long Barrow, a Neolithic burial mound in England.

branch off of a narrow passage in the heart of the mound. The remains of more than 50 people were found buried in the Long Barrow.

Located nearby is Silbury Hill, the largest of all the earth mounds made during the Neolithic period in Europe. Silbury Hill is 130 feet (40 m) high with a flattened top that measures 100 feet (30 m) across. Made around the same time as the large stone circle at Avebury, Silbury Hill incorporates some of the chalk dug out during the construction at Avebury.

Most Neolithic mounds were burial places or funerary monuments, but in spite of several excavations, no traces of burials have ever been found at Silbury Hill. Historians remain uncertain about its significance, although some suggest that Silbury Hill was the focal point of a large religious-ritual complex that

included the stone circle at Avebury, the West Kennet Long Barrow, and a number of other Neolithic earth and stone structures in the area. This complex may have been focused on sun worship or the movements of the stars, or it may have been used by a fertility cult to celebrate the Earth Mother.

The end of the Neolithic period

Around three centuries before the circles at Avebury and the mound at Silbury Hill were built, people of the single-grave culture and the corded-ware culture occupied most of northern, central, and eastern Europe. The single-grave people appear to have replaced the funnel-beaker people in Scandinavia, northwest Germany, and the Netherlands around 2900 BCE. They are often seen as a subgroup of the corded-ware group, which also occupied large areas farther east.

STONEHENGE

The great stone circle of Stonehenge in Wiltshire, England, is an enduring mystery. Historians do not know for sure why or how a collection of standing stones and earthworks was built on such a massive scale. This vast structure, which may have been a solar temple or a tribal gathering place, was constructed in stages over a period of 2,000 years beginning in 3100 BCE. It may have been used for religious rites for centuries more. Its first structures date to the Neolithic period, while its celebrated alignment of standing stones was raised around the time that the Bronze Age was beginning in England and northern Europe.

The first construction at Stonehenge was a circular ditch and bank roughly 320 feet (98 m) in diameter. There may also have been a standing circle of wooden uprights; a series of holes was found within the bank. This structure was used for around 500 years and then abandoned. Around 2100 BCE, as many as 80 standing stones were set up in the middle of the enclosure in order to create two concentric circles. These were huge stones, each weighing up to 4 tons (3,600 kg), made from bluestone from the Preseli Mountains in southern Wales around 240 miles (385 km) away. Historians believe that the Preseli bluestones were transported by sea and river and then dragged overland using wooden rollers. The circle entrance was aligned with the sunrise at summer solstice and a long approach, later called the Avenue, was created along this alignment.

Around 100 years later, 30 vast sarsen stones were erected in pairs capped with stone lintels to form a circle. Within the circle, 10 more stones were raised—also in pairs and with capstones—in a horseshoe formation. Of these sarsen stones, 17 remain standing today. These stones are up to 30 feet (9 m) tall and weight as much as 50 tons (45,000 kg).

Around 1900 BCE, some 20 of the bluestones were moved to make an oval within the horseshoe formation of sarsen stones. Then, between around 1600 and 1500 BCE, this oval group was replaced by a horseshoe of the bluestone pillars, and another circle of bluestones was erected within the circle of sarsen stones. Historians believe that the site was still in use as late as 1100 BCE, when the Avenue was extended until it met a nearby river, the Avon.

Many of the stones that made up the ancient circle of Stonehenge are still standing today.

SKARA BRAE

Most people in the Neolithic period built houses from wood and plant materials, but in areas where wood was scarce, people used stone, coral, or clay bricks. Houses in Jericho were made of stone, for example, and those in Çatalhüyük were made of sun-baked clay bricks. At Skara Brae on Mainland, the largest of the Orkney Isles (off the coast of Scotland), people built a village of seven or eight houses entirely out of stone. Even the beds and cupboards were made of stone, although the roofs were probably fashioned from whale bones and thatch.

All the houses at Skara Brae had a similar design. There was a large room with a central hearth, used for cooking and heating; a stone box bed on either side, which was probably made both fragrant and comfortable with a lining of wild heather; and a dresser and chair, both also of stone. The houses were linked by paved alleyways, and there were drains from each house running into a central sewer.

Skara Brae was occupied from around 3100 to 2500 BCE. Over that time, the village-dwellers buried the houses in a combination of peat ash, sand, and domestic rubbish, presumably as a protection against bitter sea winds. The people raised cows and sheep and planted and harvested cereals, but they supplemented this diet by hunting and fishing.

The settlement at Skara Brae was occupied for around 600 years.

Single-grave people were herders, who had previously lived on the vast steppes of what is now southern Russia and had been driven westward by climate or by other groups. They burned down forests to make grazing land and then, after exhausting the land, moved on, burning as they went. They may have been a warlike people who cleared the new lands of existing occupants as well as of trees. As their name indicates, the single-grave people buried their dead singly in round mounds or *tumuli*. The corded-ware people are named after their pottery, which was often decorated with corded impressions.

Another culture, that of the bell-beaker people, arose around 2800 BCE either in Spain or central Europe. Over the course of the next 1,000 years, this culture spread across Europe, as far as Portugal to the south, Ireland to the west, the Shetland Islands to the north, and Hungary to the east. Named after their drinking vessels, which have no feet and look like bells when inverted, these people worked copper and gold because they lived at the time when the age of stone tools gave way to the age of metal tools across Europe. Archaeologists cannot be certain whether the bell-beaker people themselves traveled throughout Europe or whether their culture spread through trading links.

The end of the Stone Age

The Neolithic period, the last phase of the Stone Age (in which people made stone tools), came to an end across Europe in the third and second millenniums BCE, as the Bronze Age (in which people made bronze tools, weapons, and other artifacts) began. Like the earlier transition from nomadic hunting to settled farming, the momentous shift from stone to metal tools took place very gradually and at different times in different parts of the world.

See also:

The Bronze Age (volume 1, page 32) • Early Humans (volume 1, page 6)

Silbury Hill, England, is the largest known Neolithic earth mound. It is located near the stone circle at Avebury.

THE
BRONZE AGE

In the fourth millennium BCE, metalworkers in the Caucasus discovered how to make a new alloy—bronze. Bronze was far more suitable for making weapons and tools than pure metals such as copper, and its use gradually spread throughout the world.

In the Bronze Age, early humans began to make tools and other artifacts of metal. This innovation marked the end of the Stone Age, which lasted for around 2 million years and was characterized by people making tools of increasing quality and sophistication from stone.

In Iran and Turkey, the shift from stone to metal began as early as around 7000 BCE, when skilled craftsmen started making precious objects from copper and gold, which they found occurring naturally in a pure state. At Çayönü Tepesi and Çatalhüyük, both in modern-day Turkey, craftspeople made copper picks, needles, and rolls of copper wire that may have been worn as bracelets.

Over the course of the next 1,000 to 2,000 years, their descendants learned to smelt copper. They extracted it from copper ores such as the green mineral malachite, the dark red mineral cuprite, or the blue mineral azurite. They also discovered how to temper copper. They did so by first heating and cooling it to make it malleable and then hammering it to produce a harder, tougher edge (see box, page 35).

Next, people discovered that copper would melt at very high temperatures and could be cast into particular forms using molds. These developments made it possible to fashion weapons such as spearheads and axes from copper. By around 4000 BCE, smiths in Iran and southeastern Europe were making wood-handled copper axes. The technique spread northward. Evidence for this spread comes from the corpse of a hunter who died around 3500 BCE and was found in the Tyrolean Alps in 1991 CE. He was carrying a copper-headed hatchet with other tools and weapons of flint when he collapsed and died, probably from blood loss after sustaining a wound, high on the icy mountainside (see box, page 34).

The first alloys

In the fourth millennium BCE, in the developing towns and cities of the Mesopotamian civilization (in present-day Iraq), temples and other religious centers were major patrons for the smiths, who experimented with casting processes and complex molds to produce varied materials for religious adornment. As part of this process, smiths produced the first deliberately made alloy—arsenical copper, made by mixing copper with the poisonous element arsenic to make a stronger metal that also had an attractive, silvery appearance.

Around 3500 BCE, people in the Caucasus first made bronze, an alloy of copper and tin. They used tin from the mountains of Anatolia (the area once called Asia Minor that lies between the

32

This bronze ritual vase was made in China during the Shang period, which lasted between 1600 and 1027 BCE. Shang craftsmen were famous for their bronzes.

Black Sea and the Mediterranean Sea). The great advantage of bronze was that it was harder than tin or copper, making it more suitable for casting weapons and tools with a sharp cutting edge.

Historians usually identify the discovery of the process for making bronze as the beginning of the Bronze Age proper; many call the long period of experimentation with processing copper the Copper Age or the Chalcolithic period (the Copper-Stone Age). The first smiths of the Bronze Age made ceremonial containers, ornaments for personal adornment, tools for craftsmen, and a variety of weapons for use in hunting and warfare.

The Bronze Age spreads

Knowledge of how to make bronze gradually spread. Around 3300 BCE, it traveled east to northern India, where bronze was made in the cities of the Indus Valley civilization. Around 300 years later, it spread west to the Aegean civilizations of the Cyclades islands, Crete, and Greece. Sailors from the Aegean established long-distance trading networks. They set off looking for copper ore and discovered good supplies of tin in western and northern Europe. The tin used in some Aegean bronze came from the eastern coast of Spain and even from as far away as Britain. The inhabitants of western and northern Europe began producing bronze themselves sometime around 1900 BCE.

In China and Thailand, people started to make bronze around 3100 BCE. Along the upper part of the Yellow

ÖTZI, THE COPPER AGE ICEMAN

In 1991 CE, hikers in the Tyrolean Alps discovered the body of a 5,500-year-old man in a glacier. His corpse, preserved by the ice in which it was covered, lay in a hollow at an elevation of 10,000 feet (3,048 m). He is known as Ötzi, after the mountain region of Ötztal in which he was found.

The ice preserved Ötzi's body, his clothes, and the things he carried with him. After careful examination, historians have established that he died around 3500 BCE at approximately age 45. He was around 5 feet 3 inches (1.6 m) tall, weighed around110 pounds (50 kg), and suffered from osteoarthrosis. He was dressed in leather-sewn fur and wore a leather-and-fur cap and a poncho made of woven grass. His boots had bearskin soles and deerhide uppers covered with tree bark; they were lined with hay and tied with laces of grass and leather. He carried a yew-handled copper hatchet, a yew longbow, a quiver full of flint-headed arrows, a leather back-pack containing oak leaves, a flint knife, and a dagger. Vertical lines were tattooed on his back, and some of them pass through acupuncture points, leading some historians to

This body lay buried in ice for around 5,500 years; the cold helped mummify it. A copper hatchet was found by the body; the iceman lived in a period before the art of making bronze had reached central Europe.

suggest that he was receiving an acupuncture-like health treatment.

Ötzi had an arrowhead lodged in his back, cuts on his hands, and stains of other people's blood on his clothes. Experts think he was a hunter who had a fight with members of a rival group. It seems that he escaped the fight and fled up the mountainside, where he died a lonely death in the cold.

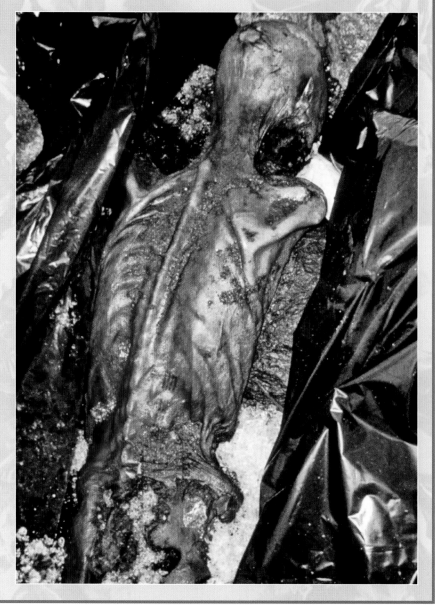

This bronze comb, made around 1000 BCE, was found in Denmark. A luxurious object such as this would have belonged to a member of the nobility.

River in China, the people of the Majiayao culture were processing copper and making bronze artifacts around 3100 to 2700 BCE. The site of Ban Chiang in Thailand was once thought to be earliest Bronze Age community in the world. Bronze artifacts found there were erroneously dated to 4500 BCE, well ahead of the first appearance of bronze in the Caucasus. However, the dates have subsequently been revised to around 2100 BCE. In China, the people of the Erlitou culture in northern China and those living under the Shang dynasty in the Yellow River Valley made ritual items of bronze from the early second millennium BCE. Shang metalworkers produced a large number of beautifully decorated ritual vessels.

COPPER AND BRONZE

Copper is a reddish brown metallic element. It is found both in its pure state and in ores (minerals or rocks that contain metal). Copper is relatively soft; a lump of it can be shaped with a hammer even when cold, but in this process, the copper gets harder and becomes brittle. Continued hammering can crack the metal and make an object too fragile to use. Better results are obtained through a tempering process in which the metal is heated until it is red-hot and then cooled off at once with cold water. Tempered copper is soft enough to be manipulated without cracking, and in this state, it can be hammered until it is hard once more.

A major breakthrough came when people discovered that the metal would melt at very high temperatures and that, in liquid form, it could be poured into a mold. Perhaps a potter mistakenly left a copper tool in his kiln and found when he opened the kiln that the tool had changed shape; people then discovered that they could use molds to cast copper tools. In the early days, the metal was poured into a rough mold, and the resulting tool was then finished and hardened by hammering.

Bronze is any of several alloys of copper—typically nine parts copper to one part tin. The hardness of the alloy varies according to its components; when bronze has at least 10 percent tin, it is quite hard and yet has a low melting point, which is useful in casting. The constituents of bronze varied with the intended uses of objects and the culture that produced them. The ancient Greeks and Romans, for example, added zinc, lead, and silver to copper when making coins, tools, and weapons.

The Almeria and El Argar cultures, which made bronze, became established in southern Spain sometime after 2000 BCE, probably under the influence of Aegean traders. The knowledge of how to smelt bronze then gradually spread along trade routes.

The Bronze Age arrived in Ireland and mainland Britain around 1900 BCE. The British Isles were ideal for the production of bronze; Cornwall was rich in tin, and copper was mined extensively in Wales.

The earliest great Bronze Age culture of central Europe, the Unetician culture, was based in a region that now comprises the Czech Republic, Slovakia, Hungary, Austria, and southern Germany, an area that was rich in metal. The culture reached its peak around 1800 BCE and continued to thrive until 1500 BCE. The Unetician people traded with regions as far away as the Baltic to the north and Egypt to the south—Baltic amber and Egyptian faience beads have been found at Unetician sites. The Unetician culture was succeeded in central Europe by the Tumulus culture, which also made bronze and flourished between around 1500 and 1200 BCE. The culture takes its name from the fact that its people buried their dead in *tumulus* mounds.

The first smiths

The processing of copper and, later, the making of bronze involved a complicated treatment of raw materials. It increasingly became the work of specialized craftsmen. The first smiths looked for

This tin mine is found in Cornwall in the southwest of England. During the Bronze Age, Cornwall supplied tin to metalworkers across Europe.

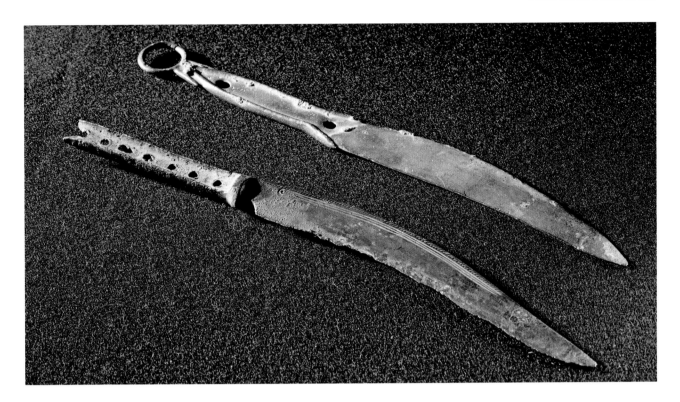

their own copper and then processed it, but once ore mining began on a wider scale, a division of labor was required. Some people dug up the ore, others smelted it, and others were responsible for supplying charcoal and removing waste products. Eventually, complete mining centers developed, producing metal for export as well as for local use.

Since Bronze Age people lacked the means to transport ore in large quantities, processed metal had to be cast on site. Modern versions of such processed metal are bars called ingots, which take the shape of loaves of bread. In the Bronze Age, processed metal was cast in nearly closed rings. Holes, like the eye of a needle, were cut into each end, and the rings were threaded on ropes and tied to pack animals for transport. The metal cutouts from the holes were either smelted down again or reprocessed to make miniature rings used as money.

Smiths played a crucial role in the spread of the metal culture. Traveling metalworkers went to many areas and offered their specialized skills. They probably followed the trading paths that had been established in the Neolithic period and made good use of information gathered through trade; communities knew where there was work for a good craftsman and where ore might be found in the mountains. While on the road, the smiths sometimes stored some of their produce in holes in the ground. Occasionally, they were unable to return, and these hoards remained hidden for several millennia until they became a treasure trove for archaeologists in the modern era.

Symbols of status

Working for local rulers, the itinerant metalworkers of Europe made bronze daggers and bronze-headed halberds (long poles with axheads), but mostly precious objects worn as symbols of wealth and social status. In central Europe, rulers fastened their cloaks with elaborately finished bronze pins; in Ireland, they wore great collars of pure gold; in southern England, chieftains had the buttons on their clothing capped in

These two bronze knives, found in central Europe, were made sometime between 1200 and 850 BCE.

gold, or they had thin gold plate sewn onto their clothes. Sometimes, they toasted their own power and wealth with drinks in beakers of pure gold. When they died, the chiefs, their wives, and their children were buried in elaborately constructed mounds with an impressive array of bronze weapons, tools, and other objects. Items found in such graves include swords, knives, arrowheads, hatchets, helmets, and breastplates, as well as plates, kettles, earrings, rings, brooches, and other jewelry.

The luxurious nature of these grave offerings suggests that, in the Bronze Age, the rulers of northern and central Europe achieved unprecedented levels of wealth and extensive control over others. Riches and power probably derived from control over the raw materials of copper and tin and over the production of bronze. Power was maintained and enforced by strength of arms—using the new metal weapons. Work specialization,

as miners, farmers, or flint-knappers, had started in the Neolithic period, and that individual specialization appears to have fed into developing ideas of status and rank in the Bronze Age.

Alongside the rulers, the metalworkers who supplied them must also have enjoyed high rank, while another class— that of the priests—also rose to prominence. Priests were surely involved in conceiving and planning the great burial mounds in which the leaders were interred, as well as the extraordinary alignments of standing stones at Carnac in Brittany and at Avebury and Stonehenge in southern England.

The monuments at Carnac, Avebury, and Stonehenge were built and used over hundreds, if not thousands, of years; although work began on them in the Stone Age, it is almost certain that the monuments were the focal point of ceremonies well into the Bronze Age. At some point, they had a connection to the

The Sun Chariot of Trundholm, made around 1400 BCE and found in Denmark, is one of the most famous works of art from the Bronze Age.

burials of rulers, for noble graves have been discovered in the landscapes around them. These monuments were also the scenes of public processions and were used for religious rituals. The remarkable alignment of the monuments with the movements of the sun and the stars suggests that these ceremonies celebrated events in the sky above. For the priests, knowledge was power. The person who could predict the movements of the sun, moon, and stars could also predict seasonal changes and give guidance on planting and harvesting. No doubt, the priests were also the interpreters of less predictable heavenly events, such as great storms, the movement of comets, and the coming of eclipses—events that might have been seen as omens.

Some archaeologists suggest that these great monuments were used as solar temples and present them as evidence for a shift in religious life during the Bronze Age—a shift also seen in changing burial practices. The building of *tumuli* or burial mounds within ditch or pole enclosures and the bodily internment of prominent individuals with magnificent burial goods gave way over many centuries to the use of cremation accompanied by minimal burial gifts. Some anthropologists suggest that while bodily burial was associated with a fertility cult based on the land, cremation was linked to sun worship.

The Urnfield culture

Arising between around 1200 and 1000 BCE, the Urnfield culture of central Europe typifies the change in funerary customs. The culture takes its name from the burial practice of cremating the dead

The figures on this bronze bowl were made by people of the Hallstatt culture, who lived between around 1200 and 500 BCE in parts of present-day Austria.

These bronze tools, three hatchet blades and a sickle, were made in the early third millennium BCE in the area that is now Israel.

and burying them in urns in fields. The culture appears to have developed gradually out of the earlier Tumuli culture, whose people interred their dead in *tumuli* (burial mounds), but much of the archaeological evidence is confusing, and there is little general agreement among scholars about the chronology. Some scholars believe that the Urnfield culture originated in the area of present-day Hungary, where some of the earliest traces of cremation practices have been found, and spread from there to develop at the foot of the Alps in the region of southern Germany.

There is evidence that the people of the Urnfield culture spread widely. They appeared in the villages of the Swiss marshland, traveling via the Rhine Valley through Germany to the Netherlands

and eastern England. Their traces have also been found in eastern and southern France, Spain, and northern Italy.

Iron weapons

In the second millennium BCE, people were on the move. Many of the nomads were warlike, hungry for land. Many communities in central Europe and the western Mediterranean lived on hilltops fortified with ditches and stone or turf ramparts. The people feared attacks by gangs of raiders. Even the well-established civilizations of northern India and the eastern Mediterranean were not immune. Around 1500 BCE, the Indus Valley civilization was overrun by bands of warlike nomads who called themselves Aryans (from *Arya*, meaning "noble"). The Mycenean civilization of Greece collapsed in the face of northern raiders called the Dorians sometime around 1200 BCE.

In this period, the Bronze Age drew to a close as people began making tools and weapons from a much harder and tougher metal: iron. The Iron Age had in fact started as early as 1700 BCE in western Asia, when the warlike Hittites pioneered iron smelting. The Aryan conquerors of India also used iron weapons.

By 1200 BCE, iron was well established in the Middle East and southeastern Europe. However, the Iron Age did not begin in central and northern Europe or in China until the seventh and sixth centuries BCE.

See also:

The Age of the Megaliths (volume 1, page 18) • Early Humans (volume 1, page 6) • The Iron Age (volume 1, page 42)

This stone relief depicts a Hittite soldier. The Hittites were the first people to use weapons made of iron, an innovation that signaled the beginning of the end of the Bronze Age.

THE IRON AGE

TIME LINE

c. 1700 BCE

Hittites begin making tools and weapons out of iron.

c. 1200 BCE

Hallstatt culture emerges in present-day Austria; reaches height of influence between 800 and 500 BCE.

c. 700 BCE

Scythians migrate into southern Russia from homeland in central Asia.

c. 500 BCE

La Tène culture emerges in Switzerland; spreads over much of western Europe during following centuries.

c. 450 BCE

Iberians learn art of producing iron from contact with Greeks and Phoenicians.

c. 200 BCE

Germanic tribes begin moving southward, threatening borders of Roman Empire.

From around 1700 BCE onward, people began to make their tools out of iron. This change gave its name to an entire era of human history—the Iron Age. In western and central Europe, the Iron Age coincided with the growth of Celtic culture.

From the early second millennium BCE, people in western Asia and southeastern Europe gradually learned to make tools and weapons from iron rather than from bronze. Iron is harder than bronze, as well as being easier to produce because iron ore is far more plentiful than copper ore. The discovery of iron had an enormous effect. Previously, bronze tools and weapons had largely belonged only to the elite. In the new era, however, even poor farmers were able to acquire hard iron tools. Ironsmiths also produced very tough weapons.

The beginning of the Iron Age

The development of iron marks the beginning of the Iron Age. Under the three-age system proposed by Danish archaeologist Christian Thomsen in the 19th century CE (see box, page 45), the Iron Age succeeded the Bronze Age, which itself followed the Stone Age. The shift from bronze to iron was very gradual and took place over the course of several centuries and at different times in different places, just as with earlier shifts from hunting and gathering to settled farming, and from the use of stone tools to bronze tools.

People first used iron in western Asia around 3000 BCE. Archaeologists believe much of the early iron came from meteorites and was viewed as a rare and precious metal, more precious even than gold. The first iron objects were used for ceremonial rather than for practical purposes. However, from the early second millennium BCE, smiths in Anatolia (roughly present-day Turkey) were making tools and other objects from iron ore, which was more plentiful. The weapons they made were far superior to their bronze predecessors.

From the early days of iron, the new metal was put to use in war, and the land-hungry raiders who fought with iron weapons established ironworking in the territories they conquered. Around the 17th century BCE, the warlike Hittites—an Indo-European people originally from the lands north of the Black Sea—built a fearsome military reputation on the use of iron weapons and established a great empire from their base in Anatolia. Around 1600 BCE, the Hittites even sacked the Mesopotamian city of Babylon. Around the same time, the Aryans—another group of Indo-Europeans—overran the remnants of the once-great Indus Valley civilization. The Aryans were armed with iron weapons.

This iron sickle was made in the first century BCE. While bronze had mainly been used for luxury items, iron was eventually used to make everyday tools such as this.

This reconstruction shows what a Celtic forge from around 500 BCE would have looked like.

The Sea Peoples, who raided Egypt and much of the Middle East in the 13th century BCE, also came armed with iron weapons. These raiders, who were probably from Crete, Anatolia, Sardinia, and Sicily, are thought to have introduced ironworking into Asia. Likewise, the Dorians, raiders from Macedonia and northern Greece who overran the lands to the south, fought with iron swords.

The Iron Age in Europe

The Dorians arrived in mainland Greece sometime around 1200 BCE, and in the centuries that followed, iron spread into the Greek world. The oldest surviving Greek manuscripts, from around 1000 BCE, mention bronze only in a mythological context, indicating that iron had quickly been accepted as the metal for everyday use. After around 900 BCE, the people who lived in present-day Italy also began using iron.

Iron spread into Europe along trade routes that ran from Greece through northern Italy and into central Europe. Among the earliest people to use iron in western and central Europe were those of the Hallstatt culture, named after a village southeast of Salzburg, Austria. The Hallstatt culture originated as early as 1200 BCE but was at its peak between around 800 and 500 BCE. It was around this time that the Hallstatt smiths began

44

This gold jewelry was made around the sixth century BCE by metalworkers from the Hallstatt culture.

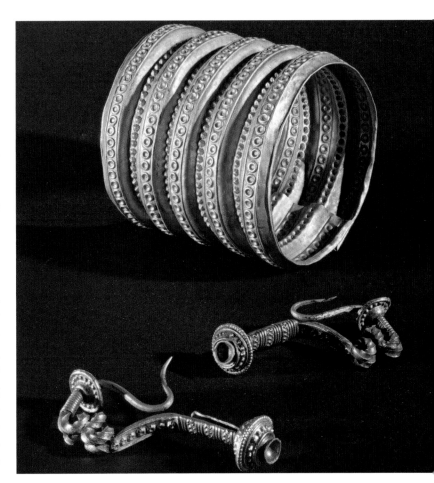

working iron. The Hallstatt people of this era were the ancestors of the Celts. In the fifth and fourth centuries BCE, they would settle all of western Europe and lands as far east as Anatolia.

The Hallstatt culture developed in an area where settlements based on mining had flourished since the Old Stone Age (before 10,000 BCE). Since around 5000 BCE, people had lived by producing salt, which was found in the local spring-water. When the water was collected and allowed to evaporate, it left behind a salty residue. In the Bronze Age, people in the Hallstatt region exported salt to Italy in return for bronze jewelry and luxury items. They eventually began making bronze and became excellent metal-workers themselves. Archaeological excavations in the area have uncovered hammered bronze pails and platters, finely

THE THREE-AGE SYSTEM

In 1836 CE, the Danish archaeologist Christian Thomsen (1788–1865 CE) proposed a new way of categorizing early human history, based on the materials people used for making tools and weapons. Writing in his book *A Guide to Northern Antiquities*, Thomsen suggested dividing early history into three distinct periods: the Stone Age, the Bronze Age, and the Iron Age. Thomsen's scheme was the first classification of prehistory to be widely adopted, although Frenchman Nicholas Mahudel had proposed a similar system in the early 18th century CE. Subsequently, further divisions were introduced to split the Stone Age into the Paleolithic (Old Stone), Mesolithic (Middle Stone), and Neolithic (New Stone) periods. Thomsen created his classification while cataloging the collection of Scandinavian antiquities at the National Museum of Denmark, where he was curator for almost 50 years. His focus was on human development in central and northern Europe, but later historians used his classification to categorize developments in other parts of the world.

Thomsen's system had its flaws. For example, the movement from Stone Age to Bronze Age and from Bronze Age to Iron Age took place much earlier in the countries of western Asia than in northern Europe. In addition, in some places, the three-age scheme did not apply. In central and southern Africa, for example, there was no such thing as a Bronze Age; the Iron Age immediately followed the Stone Age.

CELTIC ARTWORKS

The Celts of the Iron Age were great artists and craftspeople who worked in gold, coral, enamel, glass, wood, stone, and bronze, as well as iron. Their sculpture was inspired by that of the Greeks but nonetheless showed a powerful style of its own. The Celts carved images of gods, masks, statues, and animal figures from wood and stone. Celtic craftsmen made both functional objects and beautiful pieces of jewelry that were almost totally covered with symmetrical patterns that intertwined abstract motifs with stylized images of people and animals. The Celts also loved color. According to the Greek historian Diodorus of Sicily, for example, the Celts wore brightly colored, embroidered or woven clothing with stripes or even close checks; they often decorated metal objects with enamel or pieces of coral or colored glass.

The distinctive La Tène decorative style—based on spirals, circles, and S shapes—was derived from a blend of older, central European Hallstatt art (with its geometric decoration) and newer influences from Greek and Etruscan artifacts brought by traders. It is possible that the La Tène style was also influenced by the animal motifs used in the jewelry of the Scythians. Archaeologists have found magnificent Celtic remains not only in graves but also in rivers, lakes, and bogs. It was a common Celtic custom to throw precious possessions into areas of water as an offering to nature and water deities.

Celtic craftsmanship could even be seen on the field of battle. Nobles rode in two-wheeled chariots that displayed great craftsmanship. The wheels were formed from a single piece of wood and finished with iron; spokes, naves, hubcaps, and mountings were flawless. The clasps and bits of the harnesses gave similar evidence of amazing technical skill, as did the quality of the metalwork evident in the soldiers' weapons and military gear. This was so great that it was praised by Julius Caesar himself.

These gold torques, found in England, would have been worn by members of the Celtic nobility.

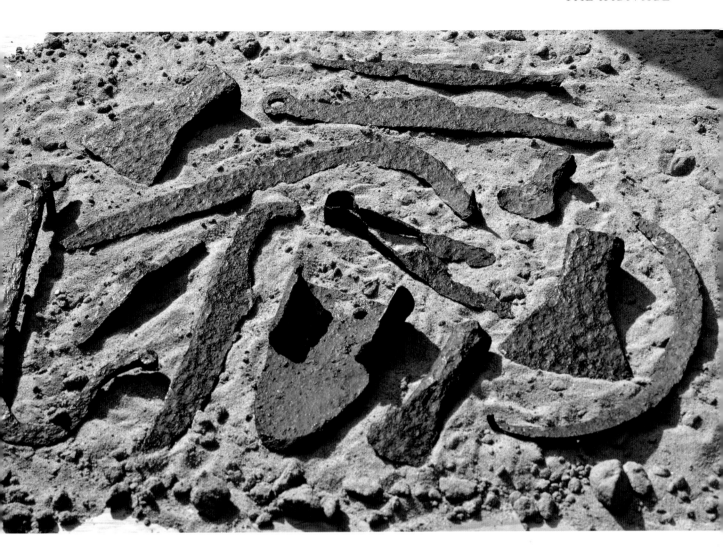

worked bronze stands, as well as bronze pins, chains, and pendants. They also made delicately finished figurines and rings in gold. By around 800 BCE, they were working iron and producing iron weapons and tools.

In their ironwork, their bronze carving, and their earthenware pots, Hallstatt craftsmen used geometric designs. Their pots had a smaller base and were more ornately decorated than those of the earlier Urnfield culture. Some vases had small, but beautifully sculpted, figures imprinted on the body.

Violent times

The Hallstatt culture developed in the Austrian Alps and gradually expanded in all directions. It spread south as far as the Tagus River in Spain, north as far as the lower Rhine in the Netherlands, east as far as Hungary, and west throughout eastern France. The culture also spread by sea to mainland Britain and Ireland. This was an age of violence, spread by warlike tribesmen wielding iron weapons, and the expansion of the Hallstatt culture did not occur without conflict. Groups of warriors from the core areas overpowered their neighboring tribes.

The Hallstatt people appear to have had few trading links to the north; they exported nearly all their metalwork and other products along the Rhone River southward to the Greek colony at present-day Marseilles. From there, the goods would have traveled east across the Mediterranean region.

This selection of iron tools, made in the first century BCE, was found in the Czech Republic.

Grave goods

Archaeological evidence suggests that the Hallstatt people had immensely powerful rulers. In death, these individuals were celebrated with burials in great *tumuli* (mounds) containing full-size chariots and treasured goods acquired from distant lands. The luxurious items found in Hallstatt graves include Etruscan bronze work, Phoenician glassware, and wine, amber, and ivory. The aristocratic leaders were apparently able to obtain the most refined luxuries from all over the world.

At one time, archaeologists believed that a vast Hallstatt burial mound at Hohmichele in southwest Germany contained silk all the way from China, but later tests proved that the material was not silk after all and was produced more locally. While the Hallstatt rulers were buried fully dressed in their finery and with lavish possessions, their subjects were generally cremated and buried in urns—essentially in line with the customs of the Urnfield culture that had flourished in central Europe some centuries earlier.

The rise of the Scythians

Another culture that flourished in the Iron Age was that of the Scythians, who migrated into southern Russia from central Asia in the eighth and seventh centuries BCE. They established a great empire, based in the area north of the Black Sea. This empire endured in various forms until the Scythians were defeated by the Sarmatians around the fourth century BCE.

The Scythians traded with the ancient Greeks, and much of what is

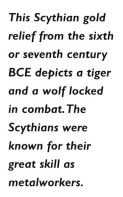

This Scythian gold relief from the sixth or seventh century BCE depicts a tiger and a wolf locked in combat. The Scythians were known for their great skill as metalworkers.

known about the Scythians comes from the accounts of classical writers, who viewed them with a mixture of fear and admiration. In these reports, the Scythians were described as formidable bareback fighters and lethal archers. It is possible that the Scythians were the first people to use horses for riding, mastering the art around 900 BCE. They are said to have beheaded and scalped their prisoners of war, hollowed out the skulls, and then used them as drinking cups. It is little wonder that the Greeks shivered when they heard their name. Not all the Scythians were bloodthirsty nomads, however. Some continued to work the land; others lived year-round in settlements that served as winter quarters for their nomadic cousins.

Most of the Scythians' treasures have been found in their adopted homeland north of the Black Sea. Archaeologists have uncovered *kurgans* (burial mounds) that sometimes comprise entire houses of the dead (see box, page 51). These vast graves of the nobility contained several rooms in which dead nobles, warriors, slaves, and horses were buried. In the richest graves, the burial gifts included objects of gold, silver, and electrum (an alloy of silver and gold). Other remains include harnesses, weapons, jewelry, and clothing—often featuring animal motifs.

The Iberians

The art of metalworking also flourished in the extreme west of mainland Europe, on the Iberian Peninsula (present-day Spain and Portugal). The people who lived in this area traded with the ancient Greeks and Phoenicians, who established trading colonies in the area between the Ebro and Huelva rivers. Under the traders' influence, the Iberians turned from using bronze to using iron by at least the fifth century BCE. Among the most important peoples in the region were the Bastetani, who flourished in the Granada and Almería regions, and the Turdetani, who occupied lands further west, especially the valley of the Guadalquivir River. Silver was abundant in the region, and metalworkers produced some very fine work in silver and other metals. Archaeologists believe that the magnificent pieces of gold jewelry

This gold vase, made in the fourth century BCE, carries depictions of Scythian warriors.

known as the Treasure of El Carambolo (now on display in Seville, Spain) were the burial goods of a king of the Turdetani.

The Iberians lived mainly in cities surrounded by massive walls and containing paved streets and stone houses. The cities maintained a strong influence over the surrounding plains, where people lived by animal husbandry and agriculture. In addition to metalworking, many Iberian craftsmen practiced pottery, sculpture, textile processing, and glassblowing. The images on their fine vases show that Iberians decorated their clothing with fine embroidery. According to ancient Greek sources, the Iberians had a reputation as excellent soldiers. At the same time, the Iberians were also renowned for their talents in music and dancing.

The La Tène period

From around 500 BCE onward, the Celts—descendants of the central European Hallstatt people—expanded into new territories. They gradually penetrated France, conquered the British Isles, gained a foothold in northern Spain, and spread across the Alps into northern Italy.

Although it is made from bronze, the Battersea Shield is an excellent example of Iron Age metalwork. It is unlikely that it would have been used in warfare.

This phase of Celtic development is called the La Tène culture, named for an archaeological site near Lake Neuchâtel, Switzerland. Many of the objects left behind by this culture were fashioned in bronze and iron and decorated by beautiful interlacing and spiral designs. These goods include cups, vases, military shields and helmets, and jewelry—including torques (twisted necklaces with an open front) and fibulae (ornamental clasps). These designs appear to be influenced by the geometric patterns used by Hallstatt craftsmen (see box, page 46).

The Celts often came into conflict with the Greeks and the Romans. One group even conquered Rome in 390 BCE. According to legend, the last Romans were only saved by the honking of the geese in the capital city. The Romans called these raiders *Galli* (Gauls). In central Europe, other Celtic groups went into Bohemia, Moravia, Slovakia, and southern Poland. They burst into the Balkans, terrorizing the Greeks and attacking the Greek religious sanctuary at Delphi in 279 BCE. The Greeks called them *Keltoi*, from which came the name Celt.

Between around 500 and 250 BCE, an enormous area came under Celtic influence. The expansion was completely uncoordinated, however. No Celtic empire ever existed. The expansion was always the result of independent campaigns initiated by separate groups of people.

Powerful Celtic nobles

The aristocratic structure of Hallstatt culture was reinforced in the La Tène period. Nobles owned vast plots of land that were worked by slaves while the owners hunted. The nobles also formed bands of warriors with their subordinates as footsoldiers. Like their predecessors in the Hallstatt period, the Celtic nobility of the La Tène era had very elaborate

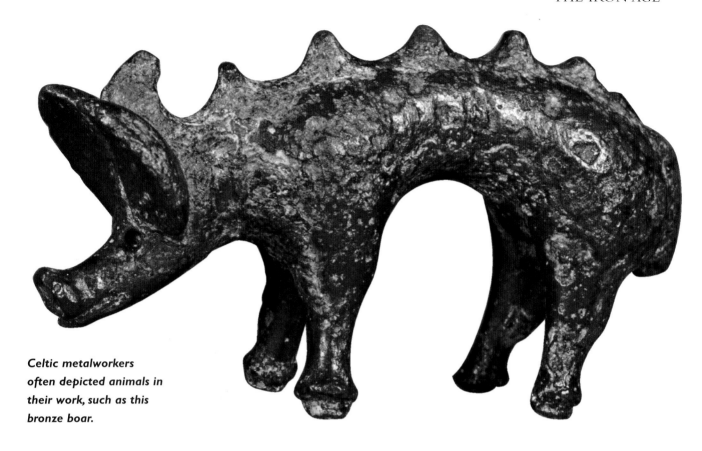

Celtic metalworkers often depicted animals in their work, such as this bronze boar.

BLOODY FUNERAL RITUALS OF THE SCYTHIANS

According to the Greek writer Herodotus, the Scythians practiced human sacrifice to mark the burial of their rulers and most prominent noblemen. The more important the person, the more sacrifices were made.

When a king died, there was prolonged mourning. In preparation for the funeral, the king's body was embalmed with scented herbs, then placed on a wagon and paraded around the region for 40 days, so all the dead man's former subjects could pay their final respects to his mortal form. For this period of 40 days after death, the dead king (and indeed, any recently deceased Scythian) was believed to have retained all the powers he possessed in life. However, after the 40 days were up, he was in the hands of death.

Slaves would dig a large square grave on the banks of the Dnieper River. When the king was placed in the grave, a number of the king's companions and subordinates were killed, presumably so they could serve him and keep him company in the next life. One of his wives, his personal servant, his cook, his bodyguard, his groom, and even his horses were killed and interred alongside him. Golden jewelry, tableware, fine clothes, fur-trimmed carpets, and superb wall-hangings were added to the grave.

Above the grave a *kurgan* or large burial mound was built. More important figures were honored with larger mounds—some were more than 60 feet (18 m) tall. At the funeral, mourners feasted on horses, deer, and wild boars and got drunk on beer and wine.

The Gundestrup Cauldron, made around the second century BCE, is one of the most magnificent Iron Age treasures to survive. It was found in a bog in Denmark and is decorated with pictures of Celtic deities.

burials. In the early fifth century BCE, a noblewoman was buried at Vix, Cote d'Or, eastern France, with a great four-wheeled wagon loaded with treasures, including a bronze pitcher that weighed 400 pounds (180 kg) and was imported from Greece, a diadem of solid gold that weighed no less than 1 pound (0.45 kg), many beautiful pieces of jewelry, and a silver platter.

The Celts did not live in cities or large urban centers, although they did build settlements that functioned as centers for outlying farmers and as marketplaces for large areas. The farmers lived in scattered farms or in villages. Sometimes, villages were so heavily protected by walls, ramparts, and canals that they looked more like fortresses. The Romans repeatedly referred to them as *oppida* (fortress) settlements. Within the settlements, most of the buildings were made of wood rather than of stone.

Celtic holy places also had the characteristics of fortresses; they were small, usually square buildings with ditches and sacrificial pits. In the Greek-colonized south of France, the Celts built their sanctuaries of stone, but elsewhere, they were generally made of wood. The Celts attached great power to the severed human head; some sanctuaries included pillars cut with niches to contain heads, possibly those of conquered people. The Celts revered gods and goddesses associated with natural forces, war, and the hunt. Some gods were depicted with both human and animal features.

The rise of Germanic tribes

In the first century BCE, Celtic power was eclipsed in many places by Germanic tribes expanding southward from northern Europe and by the Roman Empire spreading northward from Italy. The fact that there had never been a Celtic empire, and that different Celtic groups were only loosely connected, contributed to the demise of Celtic culture; it allowed the Romans to pick off different groups one at a time as they expanded to claim most of the former Celtic territories.

The Germanic people were probably the descendants of tribes that had previously lived in southern Sweden, Denmark, and the coastal parts of northern Germany. From around 750 BCE, these people gradually spread southward and eastward, settling in central Germany and parts of what is now Poland on the southern shores of the Baltic Sea. These people lived as autonomous village communities, with no centralized authority or administration.

In the first century BCE, the Roman general Julius Caesar reported that the Germanic tribes were extremely warlike, always eager for plunder and battle. However, there was little sign of this trait before the beginning of the second century BCE. The overall evidence of Germanic civilization points to peaceful farmers living in scattered groups, a people whose lives had not changed much since the Bronze Age.

Then, around 200 BCE, the Germanic groups began their armed expansion. Historical chronicles record the incursions of the Cimbri and Teutones, who moved from central Europe to Spain and northern Italy, where they were beaten back by the Roman general Marius around 100 BCE. The Suevi (a Germanic people from the region of the Elbe River) attacked Celtic France. It was one of the goals of the Romans at this time to keep the Germanic tribes on the eastern side of the Rhine River at any cost. A Germanic people called the Batavians allied themselves with the Romans and were permitted to establish themselves as a buffer zone.

The end of the Iron Age

The period of Germanic expansion marked the end of the European Iron Age. Over the course of the following 300 years, much of Europe, together with parts of western Asia and northern Africa, were incorporated into the vast Roman Empire. A new era had begun.

See also:

The Bronze Age (volume 1, page 32) • The Hittites (volume 2, page 150)

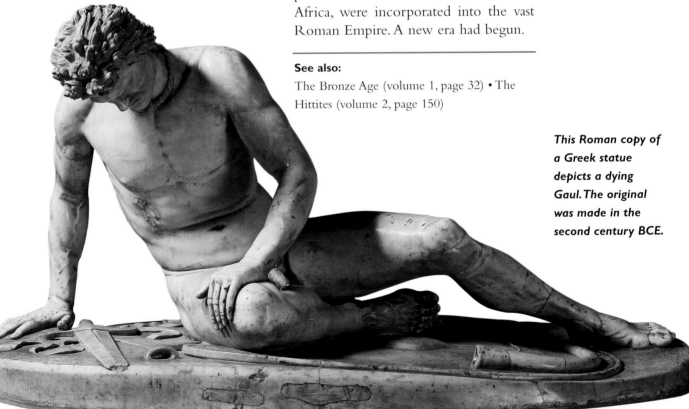

This Roman copy of a Greek statue depicts a dying Gaul. The original was made in the second century BCE.

THE SUMERIANS

Sumer was one of the world's first major civilizations. For most of its history, it was made up of a number of independent city-states. However, under the Akkadian king Sargon the Great, it was a unified, powerful, and prosperous empire.

The area of western Asia that is today covered by the country of Iraq gave birth to several ancient civilizations, including Sumer, Akkad, and Babylon. All of these cultures grew up in the south of the modern country in an area bounded by two great rivers, the Euphrates and the Tigris. The Greeks named this region Mesopotamia, meaning "the land between two rivers."

Early farmers

Archaeological evidence (see box, page 67) has revealed that a Semitic-speaking people, probably from the deserts of Arabia and Syria, began to populate the southern part of Mesopotamia around 5000 BCE. These people were attracted by the low-lying plains of fertile soil between the two rivers. However, although the rivers flooded the valley every spring, there was virtually no rainfall during the summer, making it impossible to grow crops successfully. Nevertheless, the incomers were resourceful people, and they soon learned how to build reservoirs to store the flood water and canals to carry it to the fields. With an effective system of irrigation in place, they were able to grow crops such as wheat, barley, and dates, and their communities thrived.

Society gradually became more complex as the villages found it necessary to cooperate with each other to maintain their network of irrigation canals. The settlements became larger as the population increased, and with the threat of attack from foreign tribes, it soon became expedient to build fortified walls. Around 4500 BCE, the first cities emerged, the largest of which, Uruk (see box, page 65), gave its name to this pre-Sumerian era.

The Sumerians

From around 3400 BCE, a distinctive Sumerian culture began to emerge. The difference between the Sumerians and their predecessors was purely linguistic. The Sumerians used a unique language of their own that became the common speech of their society, one of the foremost early civilizations. The Sumerian culture was strong and vibrant, with a highly organized social structure and a set of complex belief systems. Above all, the Sumerians were pioneers of writing and mathematics.

From the middle of the fourth millennium BCE onward, the cities of Sumer began to grow in size and number. Besides Uruk, they included Ur,

This harp, found in the royal tombs at Ur, has been partially restored. Although its main body is modern, the gold decorative head of a bull is around 4,500 years old.

THE SUMERIAN WORLD

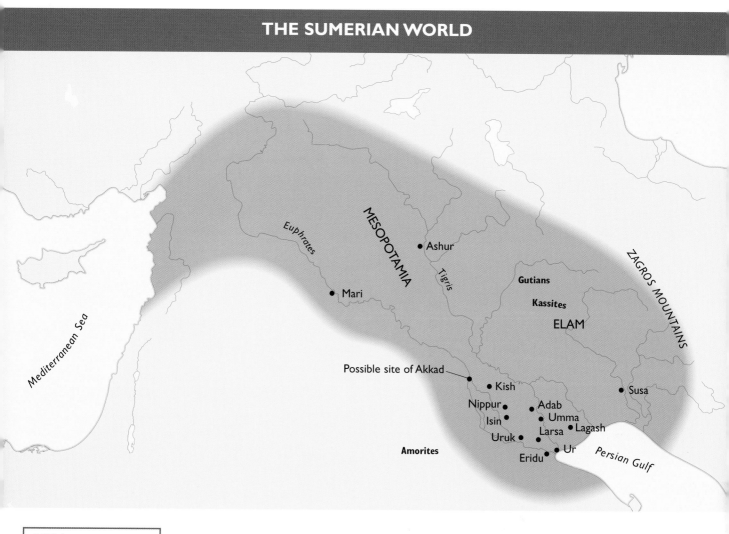

Nippur, Adab, Eridu, Isin, Kish, Lagash, and Larsa. There was no central government to unite these cities. Each city was independent, although their inhabitants all thought of themselves as being Sumerian. The temple in each city occupied a crucial position in Sumerian life. The god of the temple was considered to be the giver of fertility, and the temple itself owned most of the city's lands and herds of cattle.

Reflecting its important sociological position, the temple was the most conspicuous structure in any town or village. It usually consisted of a number of terraces, forming the typical Mesopotamian temple tower called a ziggurat. During the Uruk period, temples were decorated with mosaics. These mosaics consisted of cones made of clay or stone with colored tips that were hammered into the clay walls to create colorful patterns.

Social structure

The highest authority in a city was originally the *ensi*, a kind of governor who reigned on behalf of the temple god. Gradually, as the areas that belonged to a city grew, the cities became city-states, rather like the later city-states of ancient Greece. A new political figure emerged—the *lugal* (usually translated as "great man" or simply "king"). It is possible that a *lugal* was originally appointed during a time of war, and the position then became permanent.

Helping the *lugal* to retain his power was a body of personal soldier slaves, who belonged to the *lugal* outright. Most of these slaves had been captured in battle and owed their lives to the king. The king kept them close to him at all times, even eating with them in his palace, and they served him faithfully, both by fighting for him in times of war and by working on the building of public projects in peacetime.

The Early Dynastic period

The earliest period of Sumerian history that is reliably recorded is the Early Dynastic period (c. 2750–2335 BCE). At this time, Sumer was divided into several city-states that were often at war with one another, usually because of disputes over water rights and land.

The earliest *lugal* for whom a historical record has been discovered is Enmebaragesi, king of Kish, who ruled from around 2630 to 2600 BCE. Kish was one of the more important Sumerian city-states, and an ancient Sumerian poem entitled *Gilgamesh and*

Agga of Kish relates how Enmebaragesi's son, Agga, besieged the city of Uruk. However, it appears he was not successful, because in the Sumerian king list, he is shown to be the last king of his dynasty. The ruler of Uruk subsequently became the overlord of Kish.

Despite the constant battles between the city-states, a great flowering of the arts and architecture occurred in this period. One of the most spectacular archaeological discoveries from Early Dynastic Sumer was the royal cemetery at Ur, which was uncovered by the archaeologist Sir Leonard Woolley during his excavations of the city in the 1920s CE. This cemetery contained hundreds of burials, dating from between 2600 and 2400 BCE. The graves contained the personal possessions of the deceased, and 17 of them were much more elaborate than the others; Woolley called these the royal tombs. The graves contained a wealth of precious objects fashioned in silver and gold, together

The town of Mosul stands on the banks of the Tigris River. Many of the great cities of ancient Mesopotamia lay on the banks of either the Tigris or the Euphrates.

The Ziggurat of Ur, once the focal point of the city's religious practices, has been fully restored.

with furniture, musical instruments, carts, draft animals, and even the bodies of servants who had been sacrificed to accompany the tomb owner into the afterlife. In one remarkable tomb, 74 royal attendants were found, all magnificently dressed and adorned.

One of the most fascinating of all the finds was a small wooden box inlaid with shell and lapis lazuli. This box, now known as the Standard of Ur, bears on its sides inlaid pictures of Sumerian life. One long side shows a scene of a royal feast, while the other depicts a battle scene. The box's end panels are also inlaid; one shows scenes of the sacrifice of a ram to the gods.

A time of war

Throughout the Early Dynastic period, there was constant warfare between the city-states. In particular, there was a long-running dispute over a boundary between Lagash and Umma. Eannatum of Lagash achieved an important victory in 2425 BCE. However, during the reign of his successor, Umma once again invaded Lagash territory, only to be defeated and driven back by the Lagash crown prince, Entemena. The friction continued for generations.

In 2351 BCE, Uruinimgina came to the throne of Lagash. He was a remarkable social reformer who, according to the cuneiform records, reinstated many temple privileges. He had a new attitude toward his fellow men, forgiving the debts of small farmers and reducing the power of the bureaucrats. However, his reign was marred by a catastrophic raid by Lugalzaggisi, the ruler of Umma, who eventually succeeded in destroying the kingdom of Lagash. For a time, Lugalzaggisi reigned as the strongest ruler in southern Mesopotamia, well on the way to achieving full control over the whole of Sumer. However, his plans were foiled by a young king from the north called Sargon.

A legendary infancy

Historians know little about Sargon's background. One legend relates that he was abandoned as an infant by his mother, a high priestess in the service of the Akkadian goddess Ishtar. The child was placed in a basket and set adrift on the Euphrates River, where he was found by a fruit grower named Aggi who brought him up. The legend goes on to say that, in his youth, Sargon became a cupbearer in the court of the king of Kish. Then, with the help of Ishtar, Sargon managed to free himself from the king and found a new dynasty.

War between Lugalzaggisi and Sargon was inevitable. Texts discovered by archaeologists list many battles between the two kings. Sargon triumphed eventually and conquered the rest of southern Mesopotamia as well, tearing down the walls of the cities he defeated. Sargon then marched to the edge of the Persian Gulf and washed his weapons in the water to show that he

was the master of all the land between Kish and the coast.

Sargon built a new capital city on the banks of the Euphrates River. He called the city Akkad (or Agade), and although the remains of the city have never been found, it is believed to have been near the present-day city of Baghdad. The Akkadian Empire was established around 2335 BCE, and by the end of his reign in 2279 BCE, Sargon (or Sargon the Great as he was later called) had made Akkad the greatest city in Mesopotamia. His Akkadians and the people of northern Sumer gradually merged to produce a new, highly advanced civilization that left a considerable and lasting mark on Mesopotamian culture.

Sargon's empire

Sargon's newly erected capital had none of the prestige of Sumer's ancient cities. Nevertheless, thanks to its position on the Euphrates, Akkad soon became a thriving trading center. People flocked to it from all over the empire, bringing goods such as grain and livestock to trade. At the same time, ships from far-away India and Egypt brought exotic goods to sell. Sargon was quick to exploit the city's pivotal position. Because he

Made around 2600 BCE, the Standard of Ur is one of the most famous treasures of ancient Mesopotamia. Archaeologists are still unsure of its purpose; some have suggested it was the sounding box of a musical instrument.

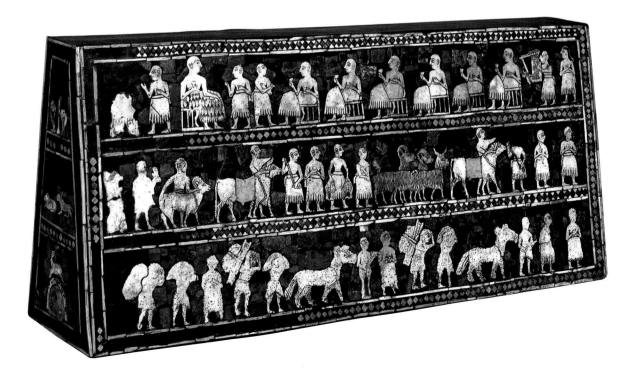

needed to procure most of his raw materials from outside Mesopotamia, he established a state monopoly over the supply routes. To this end, he took control of the upper Euphrates River, conquering a number of cities in the process, including Mari. Sargon also made the trade in tin, which was essential for the manufacture of bronze, a state monopoly.

Sargon led other campaigns, including one to Elam in the east—forcing the Elamites to move their capital to Susa. In the west, he campaigned in Syria and Lebanon, which gained him access to valuable resources such as cedar wood and silver.

Akkadian culture

Sargon initiated one of the most splendid eras of Mesopotamian culture. The Akkadians assimilated the Sumerian culture without giving up their own identity. One particularly important aspect was that the Semitic language now developed a written form—known today as Akkadian cuneiform—which was similar to Sumerian writing (see box, page 68).

Although Akkad, the city that gave the era its name, has never been discovered, there have been many archaeological finds from the Akkadian period. These finds include a great many cylinder seals of exceptional quality and a smaller number of stele (inscribed stone pillars). The images depicted on these artifacts show significant differences between Sumerian and Akkadian artists. Whereas Sumerian artists were mainly concerned with depicting religious scenes, the Akkadians tended to portray more historical events. The victory stele of King Naram-Sin, for

This elaborate gold and lapis lazuli headdress was once worn by Queen Puabi, who lived in the city of Ur in the late third millennium BCE.

example, shows the king storming the mountains and the defeated Lullubi falling down them.

One ruler

The main political difference between the Akkadian Empire and the preceding Sumerian period was the establishment of a unified government. Although the Sumerian kings had been moving in that direction for centuries, none had ever achieved the dominance of Sargon. Instead of several more or less equal sovereigns vying for power, there was now a single ruler and a government structured like a pyramid, with the omnipotent king at the top. To keep a tight hold on his empire, Sargon gave most of the important positions to relatives and friends. The title *ensi* was now used to mean "deputy of the king" rather than "representative of the god."

Sargon also handed out land under loan agreements, with himself as the only landlord. This was completely different from the customs of the Sumerian city-states, where the gods, through the temples, were the major landowners. However, Sargon took great pains to justify his political and religious innovations on a theological level. He made his daughter Enheduanna the priestess of Nanna, the moon god, and with her help, the Akkadian goddess Ishtar was elevated from being the goddess of war to being the goddess of love and fertility. As such, she was identified with the Sumerian goddess Inanna.

King of the four quarters

The old Sumerian cities did not accept all of Sargon's innovations without resistance. When Sargon's youthful grandson Naram-Sin ascended the throne around 2254 BCE, the cities staged a rebellion. Naram-Sin managed to subdue it and then established garrisons in the far corners of his empire. Having achieved control over the whole of Mesopotamia, he extended his power to the surrounding regions and called himself "the king of the four quarters"—a title that would be assumed by later Mesopotamian kings to indicate their claim to a world empire.

Naram-Sin also claimed to be divine. He had himself portrayed wearing horned headgear (a sign of divinity), and when his name was written, it was preceded by a pictogram that indicated that the following combination of characters formed the name of a god. Naram-Sin even called himself the husband of the

This golden model of a ram climbing through a thicket, made around 2600 BCE, is a supreme example of Sumerian metalwork.

goddess Ishtar. Although such practices were common in contemporary societies such as Egypt, it was not customary to deify a king in Mesopotamia, and it was not to last. By the reign of the Babylonian ruler Hammurabi in the 18th century BCE, the king was once again presented as the first and most important servant of a deity rather than as a deity himself.

Under King Sharkalisharri (ruled c. 2217–2193 BCE), the Akkadian Empire went into decline. Sharkalisharri was attacked on all sides. In the northwest, he campaigned against the Amorites, while in the south, Uruk almost succeeded in gaining its independence. After the king's death, there were quarrels over who should succeed him, and the empire disintegrated.

The Gutians

During the last years of the Akkadian Empire, there were many incursions by fierce tribesmen from the southeast carrying out "hit-and-run" raids. These intruders were the Gutians, one of many peoples living in the Zagros Mountains. These raiders plundered the rich cities of the Mesopotamian plain and were always long gone before an army could arrive to confront them. The Gutians pillaged all over the Akkadian Empire, although they occupied only a few remote regions. Finally, they destroyed Akkad itself. A lamentation, supposedly

This bronze head depicts an Akkadian king, probably either Sargon or Naram-Sin.

spoken by the goddess Ishtar, attributes the destruction of the city to the vengeful god Enlil of Nippur, who was said to have called on the Gutians to punish Sargon's dynasty for its pride and impiety.

Gudea's reign

After the destruction of Akkad, Gutian kings took control of the Akkadian Empire but proved to be poor administrators. By the end of the Akkadian era, the southern part of Sumer, and the city of Uruk in particular, enjoyed a considerable measure of independence.

In the 22nd century BCE, the city-state of Lagash also became more important. Under the rule of Gudea (c. 2141–2122 BCE), a Sumerian renaissance began. Gudea undertook an extensive program of temple building, and splendid statues and royal monuments bearing his likeness have been recovered. He was known as a good administrator, ruling in accordance with the old Sumerian traditions. The fact that he assumed the title of *ensi* of Lagash—governor in the name of the god of Lagash—is indicative of his piety.

Gudea considered himself to be the servant of a god, not, like the Akkadian Naram-Sin, a deity in human form. The evidence for this comes in the form of a hymn describing the construction of the temple Eninnu at Girsu, the city of royal residence (see box, page 64).

Despite the grandeur of his reign, it was not Gudea but Utuhegal (ruled 2116–2112 BCE), king of Uruk, who succeeded in winning full independence from the Gutians. He inflicted a crushing defeat on the Gutians, not only annihilating the Gutian army but also destroying the boats in which the tribesmen had made their surprise raids. Freed from the Gutian scourge, southern Mesopotamia soon recovered from the economic paralysis caused by the invaders, and a feeling of Sumerian national pride emerged again. It was at this time that the Sumerian king list was composed. It cataloged the kings and rulers of cities from earliest times.

The Ur III period

The final flowering of the Sumerian civilization is usually called the Ur III period, after one of its major dynasties—the third dynasty of Ur, which was founded by Ur-Nammu, who was military governor of Ur under Utuhegal. After Utuhegal's death, Ur-Nammu became king, and the dynasty lasted for almost a hundred years.

Reigning from 2112 to 2095 BCE, Ur-Nammu first consolidated his position by taking over Lagash and its surrounding area. This move gave him control of a large part of southern Mesopotamia. Most of the remainder of his reign was peaceful, and he is remembered chiefly for instituting a major rebuilding program for the decaying temples, putting in place provincial governors to administer central government, and introducing an enlightened legal code some three centuries before the more famous one written by Hammurabi of Babylon.

Shulgi, Ur-Nammu's son, ruled from around 2094 to 2047 BCE and was noted for his skills as a soldier and a diplomat. He encouraged the building of

The victory stele of Naram-Sin portrays the king ascending a mountain to attack his enemies.

GUDEA'S BUILDING HYMN

Gudea's building hymn on the construction of the Eninnu temple, dedicated to the god Ningirsu, is the longest known Sumerian text. Written on two clay cylinders, each 12 inches (30 cm) high, the hymn runs to more than 1,360 lines and describes a year of continuous drought, during which the crops wither and the mountain streams disappear. Gudea realizes that famine is imminent, and as the emergency reaches its peak, he has a dream in which the god Ningirsu appears. After Gudea has reverently addressed him as "my king," Ningirsu tells him: "In my city (Girsu) water does not run through the canals; the water does not shine; the canal does not have water like the Tigris. Therefore, build a temple, the most beautiful on earth and in heaven."

Gudea agrees to do this, but in order to understand the dream better, he visits a temple and offers sacrifices. While he is deep in prayer before her statue, the goddess Nanshe appears and explains the dream more fully. She says that Gudea needs to make more offerings and that the god Ningirsu will then provide him with more details about the temple.

Gudea then places valuable objects at the foot of the statue and lies down before it to await instructions. Ningirsu approaches him, and when Gudea gets to his feet, they converse as friends. The god gives Gudea explicit information about the dimensions of the rooms in the temple and the way it should be constructed. He promises that when the temple is completed, water will again run through the canals and the land will be fertile.

Gudea follows the god's advice to the letter, and his laborers work day and night to construct the temple. The king dispatches major expeditions to the mountains for pine and cedar and sends others in search of building stone. He also has copper, gold, silver, marble, and porphyry brought in from the surrounding lands.

The building hymn goes on to describe how Gudea himself molds the first clay tile for the temple and holds it high up to let it dry in the sun. He places a carrying basket on his head "as if it were a holy crown."

The hymn ends with an extensive description of the inauguration ceremonies of the new temple. These involve many offerings and day-long festivities. The hymn describes how Ningirsu finally takes possession of the temple "like a hurricane," accompanied by a parade of lesser gods, including one leading a triumphal chariot, a shepherd, a musician, the inspector of fisheries, and Ningirsu's architect and steward. All these gods are servants to Ningirsu, for whom Gudea has built the Eninnu. The extensive retinue probably offers a valid picture of Gudea's own throng of servants and courtiers.

This statue depicts Gudea, who ruled Lagash in the 22nd century BCE. Gudea built a famous temple to the god Ningirsu.

new schools and was a patron of literature. During his long reign, education flourished. Shulgi's reign was for the most part peaceful, allowing him the opportunity to improve communications within his realm by maintaining the road system and establishing rest houses at regular intervals for travelers. Toward the end of his reign, however, raids from aggressive tribes in the west prompted Shulgi to build a fortified wall to protect his northwest borders.

The last king of the dynasty was Ibbi-Sin, who reigned from 2028 to 2004

The Warka Vase, made in Uruk sometime between 3200 and 3000 BCE, is one of Mesopotamia's oldest treasures.

THE CITY OF URUK

The city of Uruk, which gave its name to the pre-Sumerian period, dates from around 4500 BCE, when it probably held around 1,000 people. Over the next 1,500 years, it grew into an enormous city covering 250 acres (100 ha). It was surrounded by 6 miles (9 km) of mud-brick walls, built to protect the inhabitants from raids by nomadic tribesmen. All the dwellings in the city were constructed of mud bricks dried in the sun. The more important citizens such as the priests and noblemen probably had fairly grand houses, but the ordinary citizens lived in simple one- or two-room constructions. The main buildings in the city were the temples, dedicated to Anu, the sky god, and Inanna, goddess of love and war. These temples were built on a massive earth terrace that occupied one-third of the area of the city.

Some historians think that the temples began life as warehouses for storing the harvest from the surrounding areas. The community's sacred objects would also have been kept there, so that they gradually became the locations of religious ceremonies. Because the priests were the intermediaries between the citizens and the gods, they soon began to control the running of the city, receiving crops from the farmers, some of which they sacrificed to the gods and some of which they traded for other goods.

The inhabitants of Uruk were resourceful and inventive people. The Uruk metalsmiths learned how to extract copper from copper ore. Later, they found out how to make a harder metal, bronze, by heating copper and tin together. Uruk farmers greatly improved their farming methods by using a plow with metal, rather than wooden, blades and by getting a team of oxen, rather than men, to pull it. Uruk potters invented the potter's wheel—a wooden turntable that rotated, making it much easier to fashion clay pots. Later, the wheel was put to use on a cart that could be pulled by a donkey or mule, introducing arguably the world's first method of wheeled transportation.

BCE. At first, his reign was uneventful. Then, a disastrous incursion by the tribes that the wall was meant to keep out resulted in chaos and a breakdown in internal administration. One catastrophe followed another. While Ibbi-Sin was waging war against the Elamites in the southeast, one of his generals, Ishbi-Irra, rebelled and started to appropriate parts of Ur's realm. In 2004 BCE, the Elamites invaded southern Mesopotamia and laid siege to Ur itself. Weakened by hunger, the defenders capitulated and were all ruthlessly massacred. The city was sacked, and Ibbi-Sin was taken captive. The event effectively marked the end of the Sumerian civilization.

Sumerian religion

Sumerian religion was pantheistic in nature, meaning that it involved the worship of a great number of gods. All of them looked like humans but had superhuman characteristics. The gods were considered to be human in certain respects: they lived in a house (the temple), ate food (provided by sacrifices), married human women (the temple priestesses), and had children by them. However, the gods were also immortal and had magical powers over the lives of their worshipers. In particular, they could deliver success in battle and at harvest time.

The Sumerians believed in four major gods of creation, each responsible for a different aspect of the universe. Anu, god of the heavens, had his main temple in Uruk. Ki was the goddess of earth, while Enlil, the god of air, wind, and rain, controlled prosperity and adversity and personified the floods that

The man depicted in this ancient votive (praying) figure is wearing clothes of goat skin.

could bring both fertility and destruction. Enlil's temple, the most important in Sumer, was found at Nippur. Enki was the god of the deep waters and also the god of wisdom who brought knowledge of crafts and writing. His temple was the Apsu at Eridu, and he was said to have created the earth and the people from the clay of the Apsu.

Below these four principle gods were three lesser deities. Nanna, the moon god, was father of the other two—Utu, the sun god, and Inanna, the goddess of heaven, love, procreation, and war. Every city had one of these gods as its patron, and a temple was dedicated to that god. Temple ceremonies, including sacrifices, were held daily. There were also innumerable other deities, including gods associated with specific mountains, plains, and rivers. There were even gods for individual tools like plows and axes.

Inanna and Dumu-zi

The Sumerian myth to explain the seasons involved the marriage of the mortal male Dumu-zi to the goddess Inanna. The marriage was intended to protect the fertility of both the land and the people. Dumu-zi, however, failed to please his wife. Dissatisfied and angry, she ordered him to be banished to the underworld for half of every year, which created a dry season when nothing could grow. Dumu-zi returned to his wife at the fall equinox, when day and night were of equal length and the seasons changed. His return allowed all life on earth to be renewed and the land to become fertile again. This was the time of the new year

ARCHAEOLOGY

The existence of the Sumerian civilization was not even suspected until the middle of the 19th century CE. It was then that archaeologists excavating the Assyrian sites of Nineveh, Dur Sharrukin, and Calah discovered thousands of clay tablets dating from the first millennium BCE and inscribed in Akkadian cuneiform. Others were in an unknown language. The French archaeologist Jules Oppert named the unknown language Sumerian because of the frequent mention of the king of Sumer. Further knowledge of Sumerian history was gleaned from clay tablets and artifacts found at other Sumerian cities.

There remains a perennial problem with dating these finds accurately. Because the inhabitants of southern Mesopotamia did not have natural stone for building, they had to rely on bricks made of clay. These clay bricks would eventually fuse with a building's foundations, leaving only a single compact mass of clay. A very refined technique is thus required to identify the original layers. The ancient practice of constructing new buildings directly on top of the remains of the old ones further complicates matters.

The same practice of building new on top of old was used for entire cities, so building levels became increasingly higher, forming hills known as tells. Although many of these tells have been explored, no one has yet been able to reach the remains of the earliest human settlements in the region because the groundwater level has risen. The deepest layers reached to date reveal evidence of a people who had complex belief systems and social organization and who used a primitive pictographic system of writing. These earliest inhabitants arrived around 5000 BCE and were the ancestors of the Sumerians.

Archaeologist Leonard Woolley carries an ancient harp discovered in the royal tombs at Ur in 1929 CE.

THE DEVELOPMENT OF WRITING

The Sumerian system of writing appears to have evolved out of a number of different recording systems developed in southern Mesopotamia. The original impetus for developing writing was the need to keep accounts. At first a simple picture script, the system allowed the number of sheep, goats, or baskets of grain brought to the temple to be recorded.

The style of script used by the Sumerians is called cuneiform (wedge-shaped) because it was written by pressing a pointed stick, or stylus, into a tablet of soft clay, leaving an impression in the shape of a wedge. The tablets were then dried in the sun or fired, and they could last for thousands of years.

To begin with, the cuneiform style of writing was pictographic, which meant that each sign of the script represented an object or, later, an idea. Eventually, these pictorial signs changed into phonetic symbols. So, for example, in the first phase, the symbol for a star was also the symbol for a god. The same sign was used for "An," which means either heaven or the god Anu. In the next phase, the star symbol came to represent the syllable "an," even in words that had nothing to do with the god, a star, or heaven.

The development of writing was crucial to the development of civilizations. It permitted the keeping of permanent records and the transmission of information over large distances—both essential to a civilization ruled by a central administration. The cuneiform script was universally adopted by the early Mesopotamian civilizations and remained the basic form of written communication in western Asia for the next 2,000 years.

The cuneiform writing on this Sumerian tablet, from the time of the third dynasty of Ur, lists plowmen employed by the state and the amount of land that was assigned to them as wages.

in Sumerian culture, and it was celebrated by a reenactment of the wedding of Dumu-zi and Inanna. The myth has parallels to the Greek story of Persephone, Hades, and Demeter, which also explains the origins of the seasons.

Education

The Sumerians needed to train a large body of scribes to carry out the administration of the empire, and for this purpose, schools were attached to most of the temples. Both boys and girls were taught how to write the cuneiform script, something that was not easily mastered. The script had hundreds of signs, many of which had more than one meaning. The students' tablets that have been recovered indicate something of the immensity of the task. The student had to memorize long lists of signs together with their phonetic values, plus lists of ideograms, which represented a single word or idea. After that, the student had to learn grammar and practice writing short sentences.

This dagger and gold sheath were found in the royal tombs at Ur.

Apart from learning to write the cuneiform script, students were taught mathematics. The counting system used by the Sumerians was the duodecimal system, which probably predated the Sumerian period. This system uses 12 (which is divisible by six, four, three, and two) as its basic unit rather than 10 (as in the metric system). Aspects of the Mesopotamian system survive to this day, however; for example, a circle is divided into 360 degrees, the year has 12 months, and there are 60 minutes in an hour and 60 seconds in a minute. The Sumerian students learned multiplication and division tables and were familiar with tables that gave square and cube roots. They were taught about weights and measures and how to calculate the area of an irregular plot of ground.

Other students studied to enter a specialized profession such as that of an architect. After graduation, some students would be employed by the temple, while others would go into the civil service or be employed by private individuals.

See also:

The Babylonians (volume 1, page 110)

EGYPT'S OLD KINGDOM

Egypt was home to one of the world's earliest civilizations. The first major period of its history, lasting around 400 years, is known as the Old Kingdom. It was during this time that the three great pyramids were built at Giza.

The land of Egypt, which lies in the northeast corner of the African continent, is bounded to the north by the Mediterranean Sea and on all other sides by desert. If it were not for the Nile River, Egypt would be completely barren.

The Nile is the life blood of Egypt. This mighty river is one of the longest in the world. Its source is the Kagera River, which drains into Lake Victoria in east Africa, far to the south. The Nile (called the White Nile at this point) then flows north for 3,470 miles (5,583 km) through Sudan and Egypt to reach the Mediterranean Sea. At Khartoum in Sudan, it is joined by the Blue Nile, which rises in the Ethiopian highlands.

Both rivers are named for the color of their water. While the water of the White Nile is clear, the Blue Nile carries rich black sediment down from the highlands. When the river flooded in ancient times, as it did every year from spring until autumn, this rich silt was deposited over most of the land in the Nile Valley and the Nile Delta. When the waters retreated, the land remained wet enough to grow crops.

The early farmers

Farming began in the Nile Valley before 6000 BCE, and the first settled communities probably date from around 4500 BCE. These early farmers, who lived in huts made of poles and sun-dried mud bricks, grew wheat for making bread and barley for brewing beer. They also kept livestock, caught fish in the Nile, hunted wild animals, and gathered wild plants and fruits.

The early Egyptians became experts at making the most of the annual inundation of the Nile. When the flood waters receded in the autumn, crops were sown that grew readily through the warm winter and could be harvested before the next flood. The land yielded rich harvests, so surpluses could be traded or stored in case of a possible famine in the future.

As settlements became larger, a division of labor became possible. Some people became potters, while others made baskets or wove flax into linen, which was made into clothes using bone needles. Jewelers produced personal ornaments made from ivory, shell, and stone beads, while stone, and metalworkers produced tools made of flint and copper.

Upper and Lower Egypt

Although these ancient Egyptians were almost entirely self-sufficient and largely isolated from the outside world, there is

This statue depicts two goddesses flanking the king Menkaure. It was made around the time of his reign in the 25th century BCE.

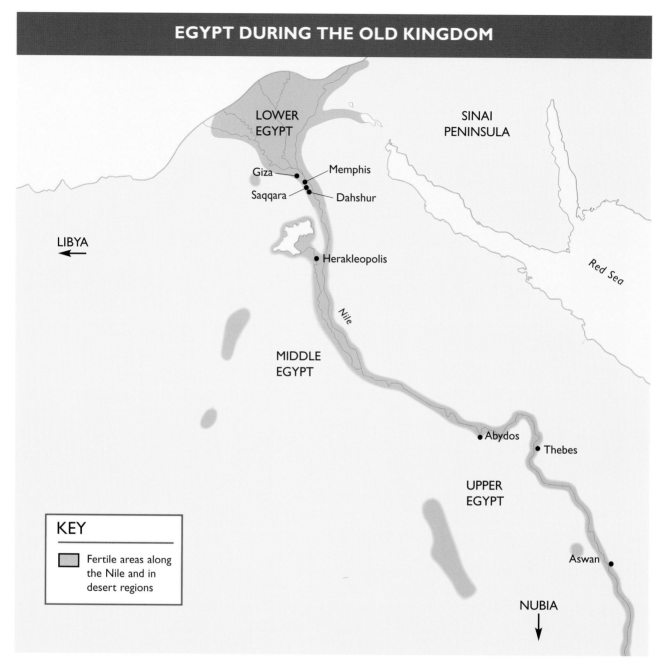

EGYPT DURING THE OLD KINGDOM

LOWER
EGYPT

SINAI
PENINSULA

Giza
Memphis

Saqqara
Dahshur

LIBYA

Herakleopolis

Red Sea

Nile

MIDDLE
EGYPT

Abydos

Thebes

UPPER
EGYPT

KEY

Fertile areas along
the Nile and in
desert regions

Aswan

NUBIA

evidence that they did have contact with other cultures. Egypt was divided geographically and culturally into two regions: the Nile Delta in the north (Lower Egypt) and the Nile Valley in the south (Upper Egypt). The inhabitants of the delta had frequent contact with neighboring people from the Mediterranean region and the Sinai Peninsula, while influences from Mesopotamia can be detected in the south. Certain types of pottery decoration common in western Asia were adopted by the Egyptians around 3000 BCE. Also around this time, they started using cylinder seals, which were developed in Mesopotamia, to imprint on clay. The idea of pictorial writing may also have derived from Mesopotamia.

The unification of Egypt

One of the finest known examples of early hieroglyphic (pictorial) writing comes from the late Predynastic period.

Inscribed on a stone tablet, the text describes a ruler of Upper Egypt named Narmer and commemorates a series of victories over Lower Egypt. It has generally been assumed that this tablet records the unification of Egypt into one kingdom, with Narmer as its first ruler. However, later chronicles give the name of the first king of a unified Egypt as Menes. It is not clear whether Narmer and Menes are one and the same. In the early written records of Egyptian kings, Menes is listed as the first king and founder of the capital at Memphis.

The Early Dynastic period

The unification of Egypt under one king, or pharaoh, around 2925 BCE, ushered in what is called the Early Dynastic (or Archaic) period. Lasting until around 2650 BCE and covering the reigns of 12 kings, the Early Dynastic period was a time that saw many changes. The pharaohs set up huge bureaucratic systems to help administer the vast kingdom. Officials supervised the work of collecting the harvests from the farmers and distributing food to nonproductive citizens such as courtiers, priests, and civil servants. This collection and distribution process entailed keeping detailed records, so the system of writing developed rapidly at this time, together with systems of counting and measurement.

An army of scribes was kept at work busily recording state business on rolls of papyrus paper, and a rapid system of writing with pen and ink was soon in use. The advantage of writing was not only that it permitted permanent records to be kept, but that instructions and reports could be committed to papyrus rolls and sent far off by messenger.

The all-powerful kings lived in state in the capital city, Memphis. The pharaoh was considered to be a god, so his passage at death into the afterlife was supremely important. Every king commissioned his own tomb and carefully supervised the building of it. These tombs were built of sun-dried mud bricks and were designed to contain, besides the coffin of the king himself, many goods and valuable items. Sometimes, the king's wives and retainers were sacrificed at the time of his death and entombed with him. During the first dynasty, the king was buried at Abydos; during the second, he was buried at Saqqara. Around the royal burial sites were smaller tombs for members of the court.

The Old Kingdom

The third dynasty ushered in a period of high culture that was to last for five centuries. This period is now called the Old Kingdom. One of the most arresting characteristics of this period was the change in how royal tombs were built. Mud bricks were abandoned for stone blocks, and it was during this period that the great pyramids were built.

The king who initiated this change was Djoser, the second king of the third dynasty, who reigned from around 2630 to 2611 BCE. He appointed an architect, Imhotep, to build him a tomb that would be a copy of his palace, but much larger. The result was a massive stone pyramid at the center of a complex of buildings surrounded by a wall. This was the Step Pyramid (see box, page 75), which set the style for future royal tombs.

The building of the Step Pyramid and later pyramids was the spur that galvanized advancements in engineering and other skills necessary for the projects to succeed. An enormous program began to train builders and engineers, while the techniques for quarrying large blocks of stone and transporting them to the site had to be perfected. On top of this, a vast labor force was required; it is estimated that out of a population of some 1.5 million people, perhaps 70,000 workers were employed at any one time on building the pyramids. These workers

had to be supervised, fed, and sheltered during the process. Most ordinary Egyptian citizens were required to work on the pyramids, but some people were exempted. Individuals in charge of sacrificial ceremonies at temples and graves, for example, were protected under royal decree.

During the fourth dynasty, pyramid construction reached its peak. The first king of this dynasty, Snefru (ruled c. 2575–2551 BCE), built the first true pyramid at Dahshur. His son Cheops (or Khufu), who reigned from around 2551 to 2528 BCE, built the Great Pyramid of Giza, which was considered one of the great wonders of the ancient world.

Cheops's son Redjedef, who was pharaoh from around 2528 to 2520 BCE, was important in that he started to identify himself as the Son of Re (the sun god). By the beginning of the fifth dynasty, the worship of the sun god was well established.

The fifth dynasty saw the cult of the sun god grow, and several temples were built in his honor. It was also during this dynasty that the so-called Pyramid Texts first appeared. The texts were inscribed on the walls of the pyramid built for the last king of the dynasty, Unas, who reigned from around 2356 to 2325 BCE. The inscriptions were prayers and magic spells that were intended to help the dead king in the afterlife.

The divine pharaoh

In ancient Egypt, the king, or pharaoh, was an absolute ruler and was considered to be a god. He was believed to embody the creator of the world and so to be an incarnation of the god Horus. For this reason, he was often depicted as a falcon.

It was thought that the pharaoh guaranteed the fertility and prosperity of his people simply through his existence. He was also considered to be in touch with the gods and to be able to negotiate with them on behalf of his subjects. So, he was the appropriate person to make sacrifices to the gods and to offer prayers to them. However, because he could not be in every temple at one time, he appointed priests to carry out tasks on his behalf.

THE STEP PYRAMID AT SAQQARA

The Step Pyramid at Saqqara was built by the architect Imhotep at the instigation of King Djoser sometime between 2630 and 2611 BCE. The pyramid was the first large building to be made entirely of cut stone blocks, and it was far larger than anything that had gone before. The Step Pyramid paved the way for the great pyramids of the following century.

Imhotep chose a site where his building would dominate the area. There he built a six-stepped pyramid that was 200 feet (61 m) tall and symbolized the hill on which creation began. The pyramid was surrounded by other large buildings. The whole complex was bounded by a wall that was more than 1 mile (1.6 km) long.

Enclosed within the wall were buildings such as a temple and storage rooms for provisions and grave goods that had also been provided in earlier royal tombs. What was new, however, was a court where the king could celebrate his jubilees—ceremonies through which the power of the king was believed to be ritually renewed.

All the buildings were lavishly furnished and decorated. In the underground rooms, for example, the walls were hung with panels of blue-glazed tiles, while in another location, there were low-relief carvings that showed the king performing the running ceremony that was part of his coronation. A life-size statue of Djoser seated on his throne was installed in a special room close to the temple, and many other statues of gods and of members of the royal family were dotted around the enclosure. The storage rooms contained more than 40,000 stone vessels, which probably contained wine, oil, and foodstuffs.

The temple in the complex had an important role to play in the cult of dead kings. Priests in the temple carried out ceremonies and rituals that were designed to serve the dead kings in the same way as they had when the kings were alive. In this way, the present king's ancestors were venerated, and the continuity that was essential to Egyptian civilization was preserved.

The Step Pyramid of Djoser stands in the desert at Saqqara. In the foreground are stone replicas of the kiosks that would have been in use during festivals to celebrate the royal jubilee.

The three great pyramids at Giza were all built during the Old Kingdom. Their construction required huge resources.

THE DYNASTIES

Historians divide ancient Egyptian history into dynasties. A dynasty generally means a line of hereditary rulers, and a change of dynasty would suggest that another ruling family had taken power. In the third century BCE, a writer called Manetho divided Egyptian history into 30 dynasties, many of which were based on the capital city of the ruling party.

The dates of the various dynasties have been gathered by archaeologists from tombs and ancient texts and are very approximate. The very earliest history of Egypt is called the Predynastic period and dates from around 5000 BCE to around 2925 BCE. It was followed by the Early Dynastic period (also called the Archaic period).

The approximate dates of the dynasties of the Early Dynastic period and the Old Kingdom are as follows:

THE EARLY DYNASTIC PERIOD
(c. 2925–2650 BCE)

First dynasty	c. 2925–2775 BCE
Second dynasty	c. 2775–2650 BCE

THE OLD KINGDOM
(c. 2650–2150 BCE)

Third dynasty	c. 2650–2575 BCE
Fourth dynasty	c. 2575–2465 BCE
Fifth dynasty	c. 2465–2325 BCE
Sixth dynasty	c. 2325–2150 BCE

Society in the Old Kingdom

The cost of building the pyramids was astronomical. The money for them came both from the king's private resources and from taxes. The collection of taxes was one of the chief occupations of the vast bureaucracy. The most important officials were often relatives of the king; the vizier (or chief minister) was usually his son. On the other hand, *nomarchs*, the officials who governed the provinces (*nomes*), were drawn from local families.

Provincial governors could also be given other assignments. During the sixth dynasty, around 2200 BCE, the *nomarch* Harkhuf of Aswan was sent on an expedition to Nubia (present-day Sudan). Other expeditions were sent to Punt (present-day Somalia), to the Sinai Peninsula, and to Byblos, a port in present-day Lebanon.

Deceased officials were interred in *mastabas* (rectangular stone graves) surrounding the pyramids. *Mastaba* chapels were beautifully decorated with scenes from the daily life of the departed.

The achievements during the Old Kingdom were not limited to the engineering and architecture of the pyramids. The period also produced notable sculpture and painting and made significant advances in science and medicine, particularly in anatomy, surgery, and antiseptics. Astronomers made a great contribution to the science of navigation and formulated the first solar calendar with a year of 365 days.

Foreign affairs

Except for minor military expeditions conducted by Snefru into Nubia, Libya, and the Sinai Peninsula, and incursions into Asia during the fifth dynasty, Egypt had no conflict with its neighbors under the Old Kingdom and had no standing army. There was little fear of invasion; the country was protected by its natural bor-

ders of deserts to the west and east and the first cataract (rapids) of the Nile in the south. However, in the coming centuries, in the Middle and New Kingdoms, this situation would change as Egypt increasingly entered into wars with its neighbors.

The interior of the tomb of the pharaoh Unas is covered with thousands of written spells, now known as the Pyramid Texts.

See also:

Egypt's Middle Kingdom (volume 1, page 78) •
Egypt's New Kingdom (volume 1, page 92)

EGYPT'S MIDDLE KINGDOM

A fter the anarchy of the First Intermediate period, Egypt entered into a period of relative stability, now known as the Middle Kingdom. Under rulers such as Sesostris I and Amenemhet III, Egypt became prosperous once again.

As Egypt's Old Kingdom drew to a close, the authority of the pharaoh increasingly became undermined by the provincial governors (*nomarchs*), who were building strong bases of power. During the sixth dynasty (c. 2325–2150 BCE), plots against the kings were common. Pepy I (ruled c. 2289–2255 BCE) was even threatened by a conspiracy organized by his wife. In Pepy II's reign (2246–2152 BCE), the vizier was said to have controlled the kingdom almost without reference to the pharaoh.

From the end of the sixth dynasty to the beginning of the ninth, kings followed one another in rapid succession. Egyptian king lists and the chronicle of the writer-priest Manetho suggest there were scores of kings during this era and that their combined reigns extended over a period of 150 years. However, present-day historians estimate that this period only lasted for around 20 years.

Few pyramids or other monuments were built at this time. No king reigned long enough to embark on a major construction, and the disintegration of the bureaucracy meant that the systems were no longer in place to collect the taxes necessary to fund large building projects. The pyramid built by Pepy II was the last great mortuary building of the Old Kingdom and shows a marked decline in both size and craftsmanship.

The First Intermediate period

The seventh dynasty marked the beginning of what historians call the First Intermediate period, which was a time of confusion, bordering on anarchy. The authority of the pharaoh in Memphis was weakening, and the *nomarchs* were becoming more powerful, setting up separate independent dynasties in different parts of the country.

There is evidence, too, that the climate was changing. The waters of the Nile were lower, and dust storms sweeping in from the south were covering the land with sand dunes. There was famine, and many people died of hunger. In the face of these catastrophes, it was hard for the pharaoh to retain his influence over his people; as a god-king, he was expected to interact with the gods to ensure the prosperity of his domain.

A divided kingdom

With the eighth dynasty, the domination of the Memphis kings came to an end. The effect of this change can be seen both in the architecture and the religion of ancient Egypt. The building of massive royal tombs ceased, and with the pharaoh

This pillar from the Middle Kingdom depicts Sesostris I, one of the most powerful kings to reign during the period. He built a number of great temples and monuments.

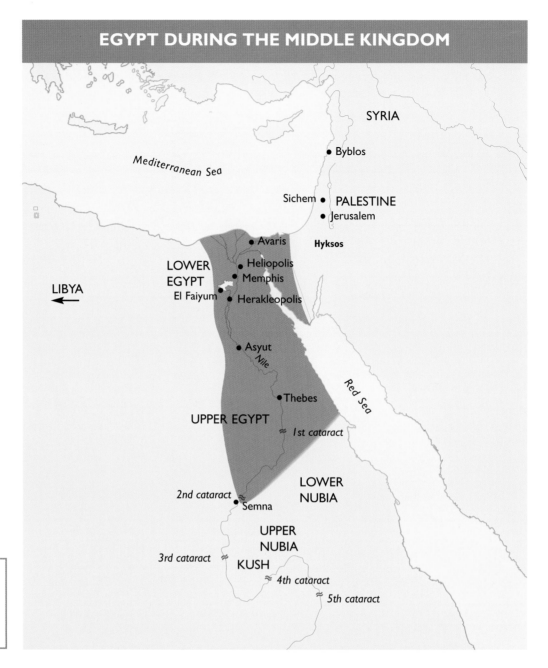

EGYPT DURING THE MIDDLE KINGDOM

KEY

Area of Egyptian control during the Middle Kingdom

no longer venerated as a supreme divine king, the rulers of the scattered feudal states that sprang up could make extravagant claims on their own tombs that they alone were responsible for the crops flourishing and their people prospering. Nevertheless, there was little real prosperity. A state of virtual civil war existed as each ruler sought to protect his territory and drive out invaders, whether from the drought-stricken deserts or from neighboring districts.

Herakleopolis

Around 2130 BCE, Akhthoes, a powerful and ruthless *nomarch* from the north of the country, founded the ninth dynasty. He belonged to an influential family based at Herakleopolis. The Herakleopolitans formed the ninth and tenth dynasties and, for a time, may have succeeded in uniting Egypt again, if only nominally. They achieved some stability by improving the irrigation systems of the region (thereby improving the harvests), by reestablishing trade with Byblos (in present-day Lebanon), and by banishing immigrants from Asia. While the Herakleopolitans held sway in the north, a rival set of kings ruled in the south. They were based in the city of Thebes (present-day Luxor).

The times were far from settled, however, and there was widespread violence, hardship, and misery. Some of this pain found expression in a new type of literature that appeared around this time. It described the feelings of pessimism that were prevalent as social upheaval caused vast changes. A sample passage from a text called *Ipuwer's Warnings* illustrates this view: "But now the noblemen are sad, and the poor are happy. Each city says: Let us expel the powerful among us. Look! The poor of the land have become rich; the possessor of things [is now] the one who has nothing."

Reunification

The *nomarchs* in the south gradually expanded their power during these troubled times and eventually established the 11th dynasty. One of them, Mentuhotep II (ruled 2061–2010 BCE), was finally able to conquer the north sometime after 2047 BCE, thereby uniting Egypt under one king again. He made Thebes his capital city.

The reunification of Egypt by Mentuhotep is commonly seen as the event that marked the beginning of the Middle Kingdom. Mentuhotep enjoyed an extraordinarily long reign of 51 years. During this time, he was largely successful in restoring peace and stability to Egypt and achieving reasonable prosperity for his people.

Before the Middle Kingdom, Thebes had been a relatively insignificant town, but with a new pharaoh in residence and with its new status as Egypt's capital city, it became the center of a huge building program. A number of great temples and monuments were erected, many of them dedicated to a particular god, Mentu, who was portrayed with a falcon's head and was associated with battle. The remains of several Middle Kingdom temples dedicated to Mentu have been discovered in the city. Other major deities were the fertility god Min, who

This wooden model that depicts bakers at work was made during the Middle Kingdom.

of a rock tomb with a separate mortuary temple, continuing the tradition of the Old Kingdom pyramids, which had temples connected to them. Mentuhotep's tomb had no pyramid, however. The temple was dedicated both to the king and to the gods—initially Mentu and later Amon-Re. Under the temple were several tombs for Mentuhotep's wives.

Mentuhotep also built temples to the gods in other parts of Egypt. The relief decorations of all these temples show a marked return to a more artistic style, after the decline in quality during the First Intermediate period.

Mentuhotep III, Mentuhotep's son, inherited a peaceful kingdom. Civil strife was barely a memory after 50 years of stability. One major event in the reign of Mentuhotep III was a trading expedition to Punt, for which the pharaoh assembled a force of 3,000 men. He also organized a major expedition, led by his vizier Amenemhet, to Wadi Hammamat in the eastern desert. Inscriptions found on the site suggest that the purpose of the expedition was to obtain "graywacke" (a dark gray stone) for the king's sarcophagus.

Accession of Amenemhet I

Historians know little about the period that immediately followed the death of Mentuhotep III. However, after a short interlude, the throne was taken by Amenemhet I, almost certainly the vizier Amenemhet who was sent to quarry stone at Wadi Hammamat. He may have seized power by violent means. At any rate, the chronicler Manetho starts a new dynasty—the 12th—at this point.

A propagandist literary text of the period, *The Prophecy of Neferti*, suggests that, at the very least, Amenemhet's accession was unexpected. In the text,

Mentuhotep II, depicted here in a Middle Kingdom wall painting, reunited Egypt around 2047 BCE.

originally came from Koptos, and the local god Amon. Amon assumed the properties of both Min and the sun god Re to become Amon-Re, the god of fertility and the father of the gods. The well-preserved ruins of a temple dedicated to him can be seen today at Karnak, a temple complex near Thebes.

Mentuhotep built his own funeral monument in the valley of Deir el-Bahri, on the west bank of the Nile opposite Thebes. The complex consisted

King Snefru of the Old Kingdom receives ominous predictions from the prophet Neferti about Egypt's future. In the prophecy, Egypt is beset by anarchy. However, a king named Ameny (a thinly disguised Amenemhet) rises from the south to restore order by force. The story was intended to legitimize Amenemhet's reign and to minimize the significance of the previous dynasty. *The Prophecy of Neferti* is an example of the way in which literature was used at this time to serve the purposes of the ruling king. In this instance, he was depicted as more accessible and more human than the godlike pharaohs of the past.

A reign of peace

Despite the fact that Amenemhet seized the throne by violent means, he enjoyed a peaceful reign. He moved his court to the north, founding a new capital just south of Memphis. There he built an impressive royal residence, which he called Itj-towy (meaning "seizing the Two Lands"). He also built himself a pyramid tomb of mud bricks in the style of the Old Kingdom. Amenemhet was determined to preserve national unity, and although the *nomarchs* continued to exercise considerable local power, he insisted that they should recognize his overall authority. He reshaped Egypt's internal administration and had a new staff of scribes educated. He reinforced the country's borders by building a "king's wall" east of the Nile Delta to prevent incursions by people from the Sinai Peninsula. He also began the construction of large fortresses along the Nile in Nubia. To the west, the desert people were repelled by means of military expeditions.

During his final years, Amenemhet ruled jointly with his son, Sesostris, to ensure a smooth succession. However, the end of Amenemhet's reign was brought about by violence; he was assassinated in a court conspiracy while Sesostris was away on a military expedition. The circumstances surrounding Amenemhet's death are similar to those described in a literary text of the period entitled *The Story of Sinuhe*. In the story, Sinuhe, who takes part in a campaign led by the crown prince Sesostris, fears that

Karnak, on the banks of the Nile near Thebes, was an important religious site in ancient Egypt.

he will be involved in court intrigue and flees to Palestine. Sinuhe is later asked to return to Egypt by the new king, Sesostris I, who succeeded in spite of the conspiracy. In another text, *The Lesson of Amenemhet*, the deceased king appears to his son in a dream and advises him to trust no one; a king has no friends, he says, only responsibilities.

Literature and history

The surviving texts from the Middle Kingdom (see box, page 88) do provide a considerable amount of historical information, while the elegant style of writing makes them absorbing works of literature as well. In place of the archaic stiffness and elaborate praise of the old tomb inscriptions, these texts are lively and occasionally even critical of society.

Many of the texts express a feeling of disillusionment, an attitude that extended to the Egyptians' view of the hereafter. Some harpists' songs called on the listeners to enjoy life on earth because only decline awaited them after death. This view is illustrated in one pessimistic story that consists of a dialogue between a man and his soul, or *ba*. The man says he is tired of life and is considering killing himself. His *ba*, which greatly prefers earthly life, threatens to leave the man if he goes through with it. This attitude is in striking contrast to the earlier Egyptian belief that life after death would be a happier continuation of life on earth.

In the Old Kingdom, the rituals of preparing a deceased person for life in the hereafter had been centered around the pharaoh. After his death, he was said to become a god, with his living and dead subjects as his dependents. It is doubtful whether the ordinary Egyptian had much hope of a life in the hereafter. However, this view changed in the course of the First Intermediate period. The ordinary Egyptian no longer depended on his king after death; he himself could obtain divine status by becoming one with Osiris, the god of death.

Life after death

In the Middle Kingdom, elaborate funeral rituals were carried out for Egypt's wealthier and more important citizens. The body was embalmed, swathed in linen, and buried in a rectangular wooden coffin. The inside of the coffin was often inscribed with magic sayings—so-called coffin texts. By providing answers to the difficult questions that would be asked, the texts would help the deceased reach the hereafter safely. This knowledge, together with impeccable behavior in life, was of major importance in obtaining life after death.

To sustain the deceased in their future lives, food was placed in the tombs, together with models of objects that would be useful, such as wooden figurines of servants, workshops, ships with their crews, and armies. Figures known

This statue from around 1700 BCE depicts a scribe called Senebtyfy. His full figure is an indication of wealth.

The gods Anubis and Ammit weigh the heart of someone who has recently died. Ammit devoured the souls of people who had not lived a virtuous life.

as *ushebtis* or *shawabtis* accompanied the deceased. *Usheb* means "answer" and *shawab* means "persea wood," so the names allude both to the function of the figures—answering the gods—and to the substance from which they were initially made.

Although the dead were provided with equipment of their own, it was expected that they would need additional food, and for this, they remained dependent upon the king. He had to appease the gods so they would receive and feed his subjects. The inscriptions on the steles (tombstones), which expressed the deceased's wish to continue to receive food, always start with the words "an offering given by the king."

The offerings were not only symbolic; the surviving next-of-kin made gifts of real food to deceased relatives, usually on holy days. The rich could also hire the services of special priests, generally connected to the local temple for this purpose. The tomb of the provincial administrator Djefai-Hapi, near Asyut, dates from the 12th dynasty and contains wall inscriptions that list a number of contracts he made with priests prior to his death. The contracts commit the priests to make offerings at his burial chapel, and the reward was to consist of the offerings themselves; after death, he, like the gods, could consume the offerings only in spirit, so the bread, beer, and meat that were offered remained for the priests after the ritual. This was a common practice.

Stability and growth

The 12th dynasty lasted from 1991 to 1783 BCE. For two centuries, Egypt experienced major political and economic growth. Stability was achieved by

LIFE IN ANCIENT EGYPT

The majority of the Egyptian people were peasants who farmed the narrow areas of land bordering the Nile River. Their lives were dominated by the annual flooding of the river, which brought water to a parched land and rendered it fertile by depositing a rich layer of silt. The flood determined the cycle of plowing, sowing, and harvesting. The major crops were wheat and barley, which were used to make bread and beer, and flax, which was used to make linen. In the oases and other irrigated areas, the horticultural products included grapes, dates, and figs. Meat was supplied by cattle and poultry and, to a lesser extent, by pigs, goats, and desert animals.

These peasant farmers lived in small villages of mud huts near the land they worked, and most of the labor involved in raising crops was to do with keeping them watered, by digging or cleaning out water channels or by carrying water from the river in pots slung on a yoke. When time for the harvest came around, the tax collector also appeared—to take his due of the crops to feed the nonproductive members of the population.

In the highly evolved Egyptian society of that time, nonproductive people were legion. Apart from ordinary craftsmen who produced baskets, pots, and wooden utensils, there were butchers, ropemakers, weavers, and brewers. Stonemasons were needed to build the temples and monuments, and jewelers were needed to produce the intricate jewelry and ornaments required for royal tombs. In addition, there was an army of civil servants to administer the state, plus scribes and priests.

Society was strictly regulated, and settlements were established by the government for artisans, civil servants, and temple personnel. These people were provided with small houses and wages in kind—usually food rations. Egyptian society also had many slaves, who were often prisoners of war. Many slaves worked on the pyramids, temples, and palaces, but some were owned by private individuals.

According to the letters of Hekanakhte from the time of Mentuhotep II, there was ample opportunity for well-to-do Egyptians to acquire and add to private holdings of land. It is clear that Hekanakhte himself owned or leased several plots of land that were cultivated by his sons and servants. With the proceeds, he was able to support his extensive household. However, the letters reveal that his relatives complained about the small portions.

Made during the Middle Kingdom, this wooden model depicts a servant girl carrying loaves of bread.

pharaohs following the example of Amenemhet I. Each of his successors ruled jointly with his respective crown prince for the last few years of his reign.

Growth and expansion

Sesostris I, the son of Amenemhet I, reigned from 1962 to 1926 BCE, consolidating and building on the achievements of his father. Sesostris initiated a great building program, constructing a new temple at Heliopolis together with many other temples and monuments all over Egypt. He built forts in Nubia (to the south), established commercial ties with Palestine and Syria (to the north), and led a campaign against the Libyans (to the west). His excursions into neighboring territories, particularly Nubia, were made for economic reasons. Nubia was rich in gold deposits, but valuable materials were also sought elsewhere. In the eastern desert, inscriptions tell of large-scale expeditions to mine high-grade stone for the construction of monuments. These expeditions involved thousands of people and animals.

Within Egypt itself, arable land was the most valuable resource. After the reign of Amenemhet II, Sesostris II, who ruled from 1897 to 1878 BCE, reclaimed land in El Faiyum (the Faiyum oasis) to the west of the Nile Valley. Evidence of this outstanding achievement was discovered by archaeologists who found the remains of the wooden floodgates that he built.

Sesostris III, who held power from 1878 to 1843 BCE, succeeded in creating a passageway through the first rocky cataract of the Nile, making it possible to travel past it for the first time. He was also a successful conqueror, extending Egyptian rule to Semna, just south of the second cataract of the Nile. The king constructed an extensive line of fortresses to guard the second cataract and prevent Nubians and Kushites from entering Egyptian territory unless they could prove they were traders. Sesostris formed a standing army to campaign against the Nubians and built new forts on the southern frontier. His troops also penetrated far into Palestine, reaching the cities of Jerusalem and Sichem.

Administrative reforms

Sesostris was also a political reformer. For administrative purposes, he divided Egypt into four geographical units. Each was controlled by a powerful official, himself under the control of the vizier. Sesostris put an end to the independence—and the threat to his own power—of the *nomarchs* by driving them from office. From then on, the court, located in Memphis, was represented throughout Egypt by a tightly controlled system of royal supervisors. Sesostris's successor, Amenemhet III (ruled 1843–1797 BCE), continued to employ this administrative system. He also

This **shawabti** *figure has been placed in a model coffin. Such figures were expected to serve the dead in the afterlife.*

LITERATURE, LANGUAGE, AND WRITING

Old Egyptian was the written form of the language used in Egypt from the Predynastic period through to the end of the Old Kingdom, that is, from before 3000 to around 2200 BCE. It was gradually replaced during the Middle Kingdom by Middle Egyptian, a classical form of the language that was used in literature. Spoken Egyptian also changed over time, becoming increasingly remote from the literary language. Middle Egyptian, which was used from around 2200 to 1600 BCE, continued solely in written form until around 500 BCE.

The overriding tone of Middle Kingdom literature is one of disillusionment with established traditions, possibly the result of the chaotic conditions of the First Intermediate period. Many of the surviving works have a clearly political slant, including *The Prophecy of Neferti* and *The Story of Sinuhe*, which are concerned with the royal house. Many stories contain a justification or glorification of the king's behavior.

These literary texts were written on papyrus, a kind of paper made from lengths of pith cut from papyrus reeds. The pith was arranged crisscross in layers, soaked in water, pressed flat with a piece of ivory or shell, and dried. The dried rolls of papyrus were inscribed in ink with abbreviated forms of hieroglyphs.

The Greek word *hieroglyph* means "sacred carving," which reflects the original use of this pictorial script on stone monuments. There are two main forms of Egyptian hieroglyphs. The first, the hieratic (or "priestly") script, so named by the Greeks because of its original use in religious texts, was widely used from the time of the Old Kingdom. Around 650 BCE, the second form, the demotic (or "popular") script, began to replace hieratic. Demotic writing was used until around 450 CE. Egyptians believed that their script, in which only consonants were represented, had been taught to them by Thoth, the god of science and writing, and they called it "the words of the gods."

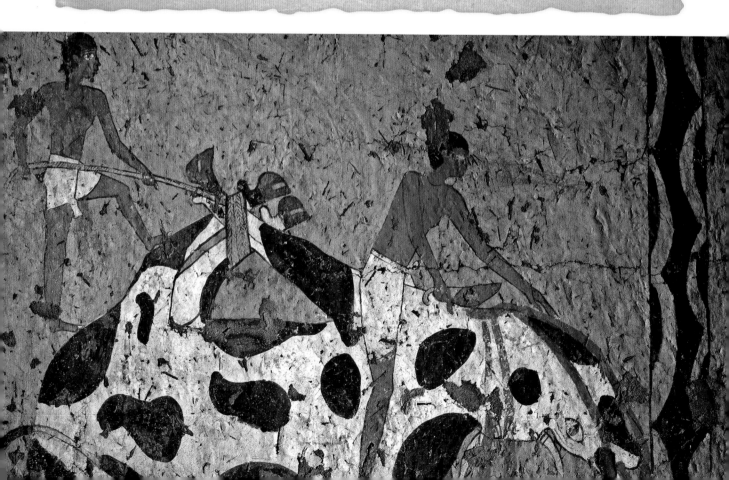

continued with Sesostris II's program of land reclamation.

During the 13th dynasty (which lasted from around 1750 to 1630 BCE), Egypt was led by 70 different pharaohs. The number of rulers suggests there may have been rival claimants to the throne at some periods and that some kings may have reigned for only a few months. The kings all claimed to rule over the whole of Egypt, and for most of the period, Itj-towy remained the royal residence. However, royal power was weakening.

North and south

Toward the end of the 13th dynasty, some of the Egyptian kings appear to have moved the seat of power to Thebes. At the same time, a rival dynasty, the 14th, became established in the Nile Delta in the north.

In addition to these internal threats to stability, Egypt was under pressure on its borders. In western Asia, tribal migration had been going on for some time—caused in part by the arrival in the area of new people from the Caucasus. The new arrivals drove many of the Semitic people living in coastal Phoenicia, Levant, and the Sinai Peninsula out into the northeastern Nile Delta. As early as the 12th dynasty, Egyptian texts refer to people called Asiatics with Semitic names. Several pharaohs of the 13th dynasty bore non-Egyptian names such as Chenger and Aya, indicating foreign origins. The fact that these foreigners could set up settlements in Egypt without being repelled suggests a weakening of the Egyptian administration.

In the south, Egypt was losing its grip on the forts built to repel the Nubians. In the east, warlike Medjay tribesmen from

This tomb painting from the First Intermediate period depicts farmers slaughtering an ox. Cattle were a source of both labor and food.

This statue depicts Sesostris III, a warrior king who expanded Egyptian control into Nubia in the 19th century BCE.

the desert infiltrated the Nile Valley and left behind evidence of their culture in the form of shallow graves filled with black-topped pottery.

At the same time that foreigners were being assimilated into Egyptian society, non-Egyptian kingdoms from western Asia were being set up in the Nile Delta. The Egyptians called these new rulers *Hekau-chasut* (desert kings). This word

This statue, made around 1800 BCE, depicts the pharaoh Amenemhet III, who ruled Egypt for more than 50 years.

appears in the writings of historians from the Greek period as "Hyksos." These kings established a dynasty (the 15th) with a capital at Avaris in the eastern delta and dominated central and northern Egypt, rivaling the weaker contemporaneous 16th dynasty.

The Second Intermediate period

The era that followed the Middle Kingdom was the Second Intermediate period. It covered the rule of the 15th dynasty (that of the Hyksos), which lasted from around 1630 to 1550 BCE, as well as the Thebes-based 16th and 17th dynasties, which lasted from around 1630

THE HYKSOS EFFECT

The takeover of Lower Egypt by the Hyksos in the 17th century BCE had many beneficial effects for Egyptian culture and technology. Until that time, Egypt's technology had lagged behind that of western Asia. However, when the Hyksos imported the technique of working with bronze, it largely replaced copper for weapons and other hardware. In warfare, the Hyksos introduced many weapons that were unknown to the Egyptians, such as the composite bow and new types of scimitars and swords. Still, the most amazing innovation, as far as the Egyptians were concerned, was the horse-drawn chariot.

On the domestic side, the Hyksos introduced an upright loom, which made weaving much easier, and an improved potter's wheel. For agriculture, they imported humpbacked bulls, olive and pomegranate trees, and new vegetable crops. For recreation, the Hyksos brought with them new musical instruments—the oboe, the tambourine, the lyre, and the long-necked lute—which were used to accompany both singing and new types of dances.

Canaanite gods such as Baal and Astarte also started to appear in Egyptian decorative motifs following the incursion of the Hyksos.

to 1550 BCE. In the north (Lower Egypt), the Hyksos kings were recognized as legitimate sovereigns. They adopted many of the existing Egyptian customs, while introducing their own culture and technology. They adopted Egyptian titles and traditions and worshipped the god Re of Heliopolis. In the south (Upper Egypt), princes based at Thebes claimed sovereignty but had to pay tribute to their Hyksos overlords.

It is possible to relate this period in Egyptian history to the time of the patriarchs of the Bible. According to the book of Genesis, Jacob settled in Egypt and his son Joseph became the vizier of the pharaoh. These stories could very well be a reference to the settling of northern Egypt by the Hyksos, who came from the same geographical region as the Israelites.

Origins of the New Kingdom

The many Egyptian kings of the 17th dynasty, all based at Thebes, tried to maintain their power over Upper Egypt, but they were squeezed between the Hyksos in the north and the kingdom of Kush in the south. Eventually, the Theban kings took up arms against their rivals. Around 1554 BCE, the Theban king Seqenenre attacked his Hyksos equivalent, Apophis. Seqenenre was unsuccessful, probably dying in battle, but the struggle was continued by his successors, Kamose (ruled 1554–1550 BCE) and Ahmose (ruled 1550–1525 BCE). Ahmose succeeded in reunifying Egypt, beginning the period known as the New Kingdom.

See also:

Egypt's New Kingdom (volume 1, page 92) • Egypt's Old Kingdom (volume 1, page 70)

This model depicts an ancient Egyptian sailing boat. A canopy protects its wealthy owner from the sun.

EGYPT'S NEW KINGDOM

The New Kingdom was the period in which Egypt's empire reached its greatest extent. Under warlike kings such as Thutmose I, the empire was expanded into western Asia in the north and deep into Kush in the south.

At the time of the 16th and 17th dynasties (c. 1630–1550 BCE), the Theban kings ruled over the territory between Elephantine (an island near the first cataract) and Abydos. In the north, the Hyksos held sway, with their seat of government at Avaris in the eastern delta. Toward the end of the 17th dynasty, the Theban kings began a campaign to oust the Hyksos from Egypt.

The campaign was initiated by Seqenenre (ruled 1558–1554 BCE), who launched a war against the Hyksos from his base in Thebes. However, he was not successful and probably died in battle; his mummy shows that his skull was shattered, indicating that he met a violent end. His son Kamose (ruled 1554–1550 BCE) continued the campaign. According to his stele, Kamose sailed down the Nile and succeeded in taking a Hyksos stronghold near Hermopolis.

Kamose became such a threat to the Hyksos that their king Apophis attempted to form an alliance with the king of Kush (in present-day Sudan). If Kush would attack the Thebans from the south, Kamose would be forced to fight on two fronts at once. However, while the Hyksos messenger was traveling through the desert to make the proposal to the Kushites, he was taken prisoner by Kamose's soldiers, so it is probable that the alliance never took place.

Kamose succeeded in driving the Hyksos back to the walls of Avaris but died before the city fell. After a long siege, the city was finally taken by Kamose's successor Ahmose, who thus became the pharaoh of a united Egypt.

The New Kingdom

Ahmose I was to reign over a unified Egypt for a quarter of a century. His reign marked the beginning of a period of enormous prosperity and imperial expansion, and it was during this era that the power of ancient Egypt was at its greatest. Historians call this period the New Kingdom. Ahmose also founded a new dynasty, the 18th (1550–1307 BCE), which was to include such rulers as Hatshepsut (the only woman pharaoh), Thutmose III, Akhenaton, and Tutankhamen. This period is particularly noted for the great military achievements of its pharaohs, but it is also renowned for its art, which became less bound by tradition and more open to influences from the Asiatic and Aegean civilizations.

After ousting the Hyksos from Egypt, Ahmose I pursued them into Palestine,

This wall painting of the falcon-headed god Horus is found in a tomb in the Valley of the Kings, the burial site of many New Kingdom pharaohs.

EGYPT DURING THE NEW KINGDOM

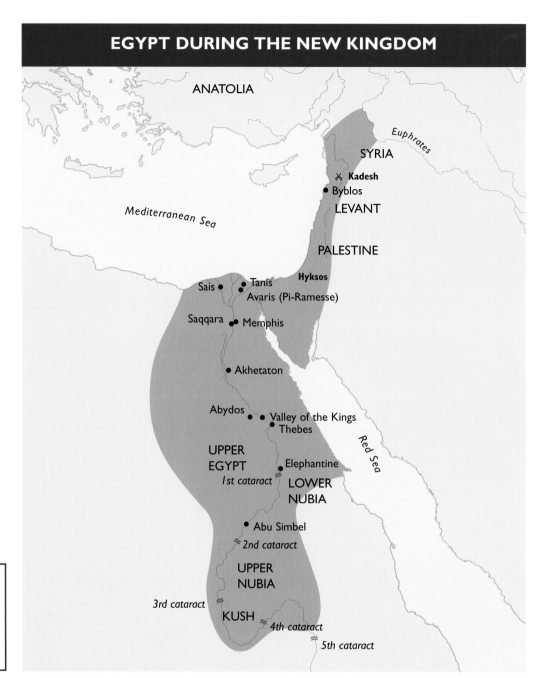

ANATOLIA

Euphrates

SYRIA

✕ **Kadesh**
● Byblos

LEVANT

Mediterranean Sea

PALESTINE

Sais ●
● Tanis
Hyksos
Avaris (Pi-Ramesse)

Saqqara ●● Memphis

● Akhetaton

Abydos ●● Valley of the Kings
Thebes

UPPER
EGYPT
● Elephantine

1st cataract
LOWER
NUBIA

● Abu Simbel
2nd cataract

UPPER
NUBIA

3rd cataract
KUSH *4th cataract*

5th cataract

Red Sea

KEY

	Egypt at height of the New Kingdom
✕	Major battle

establishing a base for an Egyptian presence in western Asia. The region was of vital importance because of the copper mines located there—as one of the two key ingredients of the alloy bronze, copper was a valuable metal. Ahmose then turned his attention to the southern borders of Egypt, where he subjugated the kingdom of Kush. For these campaigns, he recruited a standing army. His soldiers were well paid and were often rewarded with the spoils of battle, both loot and prisoners. They also received grants of land, which eventually gave rise to an important military class.

Ahmose ran his new empire as a military state. His administration was based on that of the Middle Kingdom, with a vizier as the head administrator. Many officials were appointed by the king from among the army officers who had campaigned with him.

The elevation of Amon

One day, according to a temple inscription, Ahmose, who had just passed through Thebes, was forced to return because of a sudden storm. He believed that the storm was caused by the god Amon showing dissatisfaction with his residence, which had seen hardly any changes in a long time. To appease the god, Ahmose started a building program, restoring and enlarging Amon's temples in Thebes, which became the empire's capital city once more.

The king, who was considered to be the son of Amon, elevated his god-father to the position of principal deity of the dynasty. In this new religious concept, the queen also had a special place. She was no longer considered to be just the king's wife, but also the wife of Amon. The Egyptians believed that, in a mystical marriage, she conceived a son by Amon. As a child of both Amon and the king, the boy was both a god and the rightful heir to the throne. This concept reinforced the continuation of the dynasty on a religious level.

Ahmose's son and successor was Amenhotep I, who acted as co-regent with his father for five years before becoming pharaoh in 1525 BCE. Amenhotep extended the empire's boundary to the south as far as the third cataract and introduced the office of "King's Son of Kush" to govern the newly colonized region. He also campaigned in Syria and expanded Egypt's borders in the Levant.

The Valley of the Kings

Because Thebes was the center of a great empire, it also became the place where its kings were buried. Although many Old Kingdom pharaohs had been buried in pyramids, it was becoming more usual by the 17th dynasty for pharaohs to be buried in tombs in the mountains on the western shore of the Nile.

The tomb chambers were hewn out of the rock and typically had an accompanying sacrificial chapel with a miniature pyramid called a pyramidion. The king was laid to rest in the rock chamber in a wooden mummy case shaped like a man. Amenhotep I departed from this custom and built his temple near the river bank.

This black granite statue is believed to depict the pharaoh Thutmose I, who greatly expanded the borders of Egypt's empire.

Amenhotep's tomb has not been located with certainty; he was the first king to hide his burial place by placing it somewhere apart from his mortuary temple. This action started a new custom, but the kings who came after Amenhotep had their tombs built in the Valley of the Kings.

This valley is hidden by high cliffs and can be approached only through a narrow passageway. It may be that the move to locate tombs in the valley was an attempt to foil grave robberies, which were already prevalent. The first pharaoh to be buried in the valley was Amenhotep's successor, Thutmose I. The entrance to his tomb, like that of the other tombs in the valley, was hidden after it was sealed.

More than 60 tombs have been found at this site, most of them having several rooms carved out of solid rock. The first tomb to be discovered was found empty in 1817 CE and belonged to Seti I. Seti's body was discovered along with the

The Valley of the Kings was the major burial site for Egyptian kings during the New Kingdom.

reburied mummies of 39 other pharaohs in a single vault in 1881 CE. The bodies of their wives (apart from Hatshepsut, queen of Thutmose II and a ruler herself) were found buried a few miles outside the valley.

The mummification process

The pharaohs were embalmed before they were buried. This preservation of the body by embalming seems to have been practiced by the Egyptians for around 30 centuries. The process was evidently considered to be a way of allowing the body to remain united with the soul after death.

Mummies were prepared in a sophisticated procedure. First, the brain and internal organs of the dead pharaoh were removed. The body was then dehydrated with a salt called natron, a process that lasted for 40 days. The body cavity was then packed with fragrant herbs and sawdust, after which it was treated with resin and tightly wrapped in bands of linen.

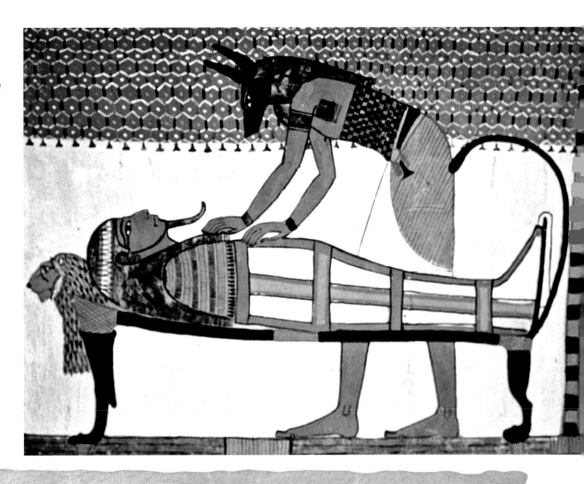

A priest wearing a mask with the features of the god Anubis bends over a mummy to perform a pre-burial ritual. This painting dates to around 1200 BCE.

SERVANTS IN THE PLACE OF TRUTH

Texts discovered near the Valley of the Kings contain an account of the lives of the workers who built the tombs in the valley. The workers were housed in a village nearby, and some of those houses are still recognizable in the present-day village of Deir el-Medina. The workers were called "Servants in the Place of Truth," and from the limestone tablets and fragments of papyrus that were discovered at Deir el-Medina, it is possible to construct a vivid picture of the workers' lives.

The documents contain reports, letters, lists of absentees, contracts, invoices, wills, and other administrative records, as well as educational, literary, and magical texts. The documents describe a privileged group of artisans who were engaged in building and decorating royal tombs on a full-time basis. Their wages were paid by the government in the form of rations, and their managers were directly accountable to the vizier, who visited the valley to inspect their work at regular intervals.

The texts also reveal a good deal about the local economy and the trading, borrowing, and lending that took place among the villagers. All goods had fixed prices, expressed in quantities of grain or silver, but were actually paid for in kind. Any dispute about a transaction could be submitted to the local council, where judgment was pronounced by a group of important villagers. There is also a record of the earliest known strikes in history. When there were delays in the distribution of rations during and after the reign of Ramses III, the workers put down their tools and marched in protest to show their displeasure and their hunger.

This wall painting from the time of the 18th dynasty depicts a scribe hunting gazelles from a chariot.

The rule of Hatshepsut

Six years into the reign of Thutmose III, Hatshepsut arranged to have herself proclaimed pharaoh. According to one version of the story, she saw the statue of Amon move toward her during a procession and took that as a sign that he had selected her to rule. Thutmose II had earlier claimed to be selected by a similar process when he was not the only candidate for the throne.

Because, according to tradition, a woman could not succeed to the throne, Hatshepsut and Thutmose III reigned jointly. Their names are both inscribed in a cartouche, an oval frame in which the names of Egyptian kings were recorded, but it is clear that Hatshepsut played the dominant role.

Even though the Hyksos had been expelled from the realm more than half a century earlier, Hatshepsut claimed that it was only her rule that had put an end to the chaos of the Hyksos era. In order to celebrate this achievement, Hatshepsut embarked on a great building program to glorify her reign, including obelisks in Karnak and a magnificent funerary temple in Deir el-Bahri.

Foreign affairs

In the reliefs and the statues of her, Hatshepsut is depicted as a man, to comply with the traditional concept of the ruler being male. She is sometimes shown as an army commander, though it is doubtful that any campaigns were waged during her reign. She did, however, organize expeditions abroad, including a voyage to the African country of Punt (present-day Somalia). Reliefs in her funerary temple show pictures of the trip—the wife of a local king, houses built on stilts, and the returning ships laden with the spoils of the trip, including incense, myrrh, and exotic objects.

After Hatshepsut's death in 1458, BCE, Thutmose III became the sole

Expanding the empire

The successor to Amenhotep I was Thutmose I, who was no relation to the former pharaoh but had been a general in his army. Thutmose (ruled c. 1504–1492 BCE) was a warrior-king who extended Egypt's borders. He occupied and subdued the whole of the Levant, establishing his furthest frontier on the Euphrates River. In the south, he conquered Upper Nubia and occupied Kush as far south as the fourth cataract. By the end of his reign, the New Kingdom had reached its greatest extent. Egypt's new territories made a huge contribution to its enormous wealth.

In 1492 BCE, Thutmose II succeeded his father. Because he was only the son of a minor wife, Thutmose married his half sister Hatshepsut to consolidate his claim to the throne. On Thutmose's death, around 1479 BCE, Thutmose III, who was still a child, ascended the throne. He ruled the country nominally, while his stepmother Hatshepsut acted as regent.

monarch. Perhaps angry at the way his stepmother had kept him in the background, he had her name and image obliterated from a number of prominent monuments.

During Hatshepsut's reign, the whole of the Near East had been in turmoil. The migrations that had brought the Hyksos to Egypt had also fostered the development of new kingdoms in northern Mesopotamia, particularly those of the Mitanni. The stability of Egyptian rule was threatened by these new kingdoms and by powerful Syrian princes. Thutmose launched a series of campaigns to protect his Asian lands, successfully consolidating his position in the Levant and Syria. His expeditions are portrayed on the temple walls at Karnak.

When Thutmose was unable to subdue the Mitanni, however, he formed an alliance with them. This alliance was later reinforced by marriage through several generations; Thutmose and his successors, Amenhotep II, Thutmose IV, and Amenhotep III, all took Mitanni princesses as brides.

Both Amenhotep II (ruled 1427–1401 BCE) and Thutmose IV (ruled 1401–1391 BCE) maintained the empire by using diplomatic and military means. They succeeded in maintaining a balance of power with their neighbors, but two new kingdoms were on the rise—those of the Assyrians and the Hittites.

New Kingdom society

At the apex of Egyptian society was the pharaoh. He was both the political and religious leader. As such, he remained aloof from his people. He was believed to be in contact with the gods, which was said to guarantee the country's prosperity. The pharaoh was the guardian of mankind, the lawmaker and military commander, and he maintained order on earth and throughout the universe. As long as that order—called *ma'at* in Egyptian—was not disrupted in any way, the world would continue to exist.

The pharaoh made laws and issued decrees after consultation with his officials. However, in practice, much of the responsibility for legislation rested on his highest administrators, especially the vizier. The office of vizier carried an enormous administrative burden. In the tomb of Rekhmire, who was vizier under Hatshepsut and Thutmose III, an extensive job description of that office has been preserved. It is referred to as a "bitter task." The long enumeration of his duties shows that the vizier was responsible for maintaining order in the royal court and for controlling taxation, the royal treasuries, and the grain silos. He was also required to supervise the lower administrators and, if necessary, to punish them for failure to perform their duties.

The majority of the population worked in agriculture, which was the basis of the Egyptian economy. There were many other occupations and professions, however. There were large groups of civil servants, priests, craftsmen, and army officers. Because of the regular military campaigns of the New Kingdom, it was necessary to keep a standing army ready for action. Within the army, there were two main ranks, those of infantryman and charioteer. The

This cosmetic spoon, made around the time of the 18th and 19th dynasties, depicts a young woman carrying an amphora.

Created around 1350 BCE, this relief depicts the pharaoh Akhenaton making an offering to the sun god Aton. During Akenaton's reign, the worship of Aton replaced that of all other gods.

the New Kingdom, was designed to allow for continuous expansion. The main plan of a temple was one of halls and open courts surrounded by impressive colonnades. At its core was the sanctum, where the image of the god resided and was cared for by the priests, acting as representatives of the king. Only the highest priests were allowed to enter this most sacred part of the temple. Major temples, such as those at Karnak and Luxor, would be enlarged by adding new halls or courts to the existing ones, all forming a straight line from the sanctum to the pylon (the temple gate).

The cost of the upkeep of the temples was considerable. Substantial resources were needed to pay for the requisite religious sacrifices, to feed the temple employees (who included civil servants and workmen as well as priests), and to maintain the sanctuary itself. The pharaoh supplied these resources in the form of arable land, grassland, and cattle. In addition to this basic income, the temple would receive regular gifts of valuable objects that the king brought back from his campaigns or trading expeditions. The wars of Thutmose III, for example, contributed hundreds of pounds of gold and silver to the temple of Amon in Thebes.

The priests serving in the temples were all sons of important and influential families. To be a priest was, for the most part, an honorary position that could be held by officials in addition to their normal administrative duties, providing them with an extra source of income. The office of priest, together with its salary, was usually passed on from father to son. It was important for the king to cultivate the goodwill of the families of priests and high-ranking officials. By his careful attendance to the temples, the pharaoh both placated the gods and secured a loyal staff of civil servants throughout the country.

commander-in-chief was the pharaoh. In preparation for this role, young princes were taught how to manage horses, chariots, and weapons from an early age.

Priests and temples

It was one of the duties of the pharaoh to appease the gods regularly by offering sacrifices in the temples. It was also his duty to build and expand the temples of the gods. The classical form of the Egyptian temple, which was the style of

The Amarna period

During the reign of Amenhotep III (ruled 1391–1353 BCE), Egypt reached the peak of its power and prestige. Its enormous wealth rested on its agricultural production, on international trade, and on the gold mined in its Nubian territories. Egypt was considered to be an inexhaustible source of gold at this time, and gold was freely used to ratify political treaties with foreign kings.

Amenhotep's reign was an era of great architectural works. Amenhotep built temples in Thebes and Nubia, and on the western bank of the Nile, near Luxor, he constructed both an enormous funerary temple and a new palace facing an artificial lake. Amenhotep's foreign policy relied mainly on negotiation, and his long reign was largely peaceful. Some of his diplomatic correspondence has been preserved on 400 clay tablets known as the Amarna Letters.

Amenhotep IV (ruled 1353–1335 BCE) is chiefly remembered for the major religious reformation that he introduced. To the consternation of the priests of Amon, Amenhotep decreed that the sun god Re (Re-Harakhte of Heliopolis) should be the sole god in

THE AMARNA LETTERS

When Akhenaton's capital city Akhetaton was abandoned around 1335 BCE, many things were left behind, including an archive of royal correspondence. This archive contained some 400 clay tablets inscribed in Babylonian, which was the predominant international language in western Asia in the 14th century BCE.

The tablets were found in 1887 CE by a peasant in the city of Tel el Amarna, which is on the site of the ancient Egyptian city of Akhetaton. The tablets have provided historians with important information about the Amarna period.

The tablets contain part of the correspondence between foreign rulers and the pharaohs Amenhotep III and his son and successor Amenhotep IV, who later became known as Akhenaton. The foreign rulers included the kings of Babylon, Assyria, and Mitanni, all of whom regarded the pharaoh as their equal and addressed him as "my brother." The rulers of city-states in the region of present-day Lebanon, Palestine, and Israel adopted a more deferential tone. These small princes were unpredictable factors in the power game, because they would ally themselves first with one major power and then with another.

The letters clearly show how the older states were being exposed to new threats. These threats included the great Hittite Empire, which was one of the earliest civilizations in Anatolia (roughly present-day Turkey) and was constantly seeking to extend its territories. Another threat was posed by the roaming Chabiru tribes, who may have been the Hebrews of the Bible. Some of the letters describe how a former vassal of Egypt, Abdi-Ashirta of Amurru, formed an alliance with the Chabiru and later with the Hittites. On the other hand, King Rib-Addi of Byblos remained loyal to the pharaoh and repeatedly wrote to the Egyptian king urging him to send troops quickly to prevent Abdi-Ashirta and other kings from joining forces against Egypt.

In addition to the political information they contain, the letters are valuable for the light they shed on the language of the time. The Canaanite writers did not use pure Babylonian; they used a mixture of Babylonian and their own language. The suffixes of the verbs used by these writers greatly resemble those of the much later Hebrew of the Bible, so the Amarna Letters provide a valuable link in tracing the development of this language.

This relief from a stele depicts the pharaoh Akhenaton and his wife and children. Above is the sun god Aton.

Egyptian religion. It was not unusual for one god to be considered preeminent, but Amenhotep's unprecedented decree denied the existence of any other divinities, bringing monotheism to Egypt. The temples of the old gods were abandoned, and their images were smashed.

Amenhotep also decreed that the god should be worshipped under a new name, Aton (or Aten), meaning "the disc of the sun." He changed his own name to Akhenaton (meaning "Servant of Aton")

and, as the son of Aton, announced that he was the only prophet of the new religion. This major religious change was marked by the celebration of the *sed* (or royal jubilee) in the fourth year after Akhenaton's accession, although the jubilee traditionally did not take place until the 30th year of a pharaoh's reign.

Aton was portrayed as the disk of the sun, a glowing circle devoid of all human features. This was a symbol taken from earlier depictions of Re. Images from

Akhenaton's time show the disk with long radiating rays that end in hands holding the ankh—the symbol of life. Akhenaton bestowed royal status on the god by writing his name in cartouches, the pictorial oval frames that were reserved for the names of royalty.

The pharaoh had a special temple built for Aton at Karnak, and to honor the god further, Akhenaton left Thebes and built a new capital city called Akhetaton (meaning "Aton's Horizon") near present-day Tel el Amarna in central Egypt. From the evidence of the stone monuments that mark the city limits, it dates from the sixth year of his reign. It served as the country's capital until Akhenaton's death. The royal court that took up residence in the new city consisted mainly of new people. Akhenaton may have wanted to distance himself from the former priests and officials.

The Armana period lasted through the end of the 18th dynasty. However, the period was so reviled by Egyptian historians that the names of Akhenaton and his immediate successors were left out of the official royal lists. In one very rare case where Akhenaton is mentioned, he is called the "Enemy from Akhetaton."

Art and letters

There were many other changes during Akhenaton's reign in addition to the religious reformation. In art, many of the traditional conventions were abandoned, and things were portrayed more realistically, particularly the human figure. The surviving pictures of Akhenaton are very unflattering. They show a man with a narrow face, a potbelly, wide hips, and matchstick legs. In contrast, a bust of Akhenaton's wife Nefertiti depicts a woman of extraordinary beauty.

In literature, some forms of the spoken language were introduced, and the variation now known as Late Egyptian emerged as the standard written language

around 1380 BCE. It was used for business and some priestly documents until around 700 BCE. Classic Middle Egyptian continued to be used in religious texts.

The evidence of the Amarna Letters shows that Akhenaton maintained con-

This is a copy of a bust depicting Nefertiti, wife of Akhenaton.

tacts with other states through correspondence and the exchange of gifts, but it is clear that he failed to take decisive military action when Egypt began to lose its influence in the Syro-Palestinian region. There were also difficulties at home, caused by the closing of the temples, which effectively transferred the property of the temples to the pharaoh. Without the help of the local temple officials, it proved difficult to collect the income that arose from this property.

The mask of Tutankhamen from 1323 BCE is ancient Egypt's greatest treasure, but Tutankhamen was a relatively minor ruler.

Tutankhamen

Smenkhkare (ruled 1335–1332 BCE) reversed the religious reformation carried out by his predecessor and began building temples again in Thebes. He was succeeded after a brief reign by the nine-year-old Tutankhaten, who married Akhenaton's daughter Ankhesenaten and completed the break with the Aton cult by returning the capital to Memphis and by repairing and rebuilding the abandoned temples throughout the country. The pharaoh also marked the break with the past symbolically by changing his own name to Tutankhamen and that of his wife to Ankhesenamen.

Tutankhamen died young and was buried in a small, exquisitely decorated tomb in the Valley of the Kings. It seems that this tomb may have been forgotten, possibly due to the erasure of the Amarna period from the Egyptian memory. At any rate, it escaped the plundering suffered by all the other royal graves and was discovered virtually untouched in 1922 CE by the British archaeologists Howard Carter and Lord Carnarvon. Like the other royal tombs, its walls were covered with carved and painted hieroglyphics and representational scenes. Although it had apparently been robbed twice, it still held more than 5,000 items.

Power struggle

When he died at the age of 18 in 1323 BCE, Tutankhamen left a grieving widow, Ankhesenamen, and a throne that immediately became the stake in a power struggle. In the absence of a male heir, it seemed that the successor was bound to be a high-ranking official. Two possible candidates were Aya, an old official who had served Akhenaton, and a general, Horemheb. Rather than accepting either of them as her husband and the new pharaoh, Ankhesenamen wrote to the Hittite king Suppiluliumas, asking for one of his sons to ascend the Egyptian

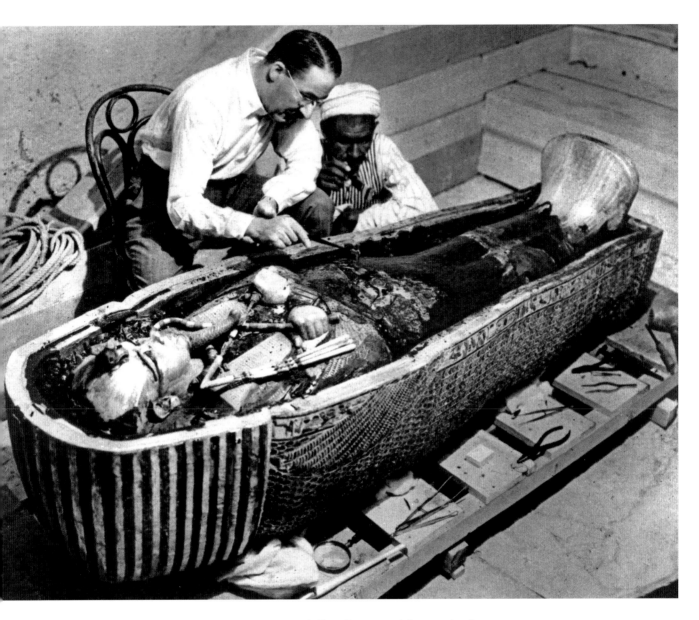

throne. Suppiluliumas sent his son Zannanza, but the boy was assassinated before he reached Egypt, an act that may have been ordered by Aya, who promptly took the throne and sent Horemheb north to repel the incensed Hittites.

Aya lived for only another four years, and then Horemheb came to power in 1319 BCE. During his reign, he concentrated on domestic issues. He introduced reforms in the army and in the judicial system, and he reorganized the collection of taxes. Horemheb died around 1292 BCE, and his death marked the end of the 18th dynasty.

The Ramesside period

The first king of the 19th dynasty was Ramses I, who had been a general in Horemheb's army and had been appointed by him as his successor. After a short reign of two years, Ramses died and was succeeded by his son, Seti I (ruled 1290–1279 BCE).

Seti led successful military campaigns to restore Egypt's authority in Syria and Palestine and defeated tribes from the Libyan desert that were threatening Egypt's delta. A military engagement with the powerful Hittites ended in a treaty. At home, Seti began the construc-

Archaeologist Howard Carter (left) examines the innermost coffin of Tutankhamen in 1922 CE.

tion of a great hall for the temple of Amon at Karnak, and in the city of Abydos, he built a magnificent temple of white limestone (decorated with delicately painted reliefs), dedicated to himself and the god Osiris. He was succeeded by his son Ramses II.

Ramses II (ruled 1279–1213 BCE) continued his father's attempts to regain control of parts of Africa and western Asia that had been held by Egypt in previous centuries. The northern border, which continued to be threatened by the Hittites, was his main source of concern. The Hittites had occupied the city of Kadesh in Syria. In 1275 BCE, Ramses fought the Hittites at the Battle of Kadesh in an attempt to regain that territory. Scenes from the battle as portrayed on temple walls give the impression that the Egyptians were victorious, but the result was inconclusive. Ramses continued his campaign against the Hittites for the next 15 years, eventually concluding a treaty with them. The peace was ratified by a marriage between Ramses and a Hittite princess.

At home, Ramses proved to be an energetic builder of temples and monuments. He expanded the temple at Luxor and finished the great hall begun by his father in the temple of Amon at Karnak. He built a temple for himself at Abydos and an enormous mortuary temple at Thebes. New monuments were constructed in Nubia with colossal statues of himself. The best known of these is the rock-hewn temple of Abu Simbel. He also built a new capital in the eastern delta called Pi-Ramesse.

The Sea Peoples

Ramses was succeeded by his 13th son, Merneptah (ruled 1213–1204 BCE), who inherited an empire whose western approaches were being threatened by the Libyans. There was also a new threat from the north from the so-called Sea Peoples, who consisted of a number of groups that menaced the eastern Mediterranean coast. In the fifth year of Merneptah's reign, he fought off an invasion by the Libyans and Sea Peoples in the western delta, taking many captives who were later conscripted into the Egyptian army.

After Merneptah died in 1204 BCE, various members of the royal family competed to win the succession, resulting in a chaotic period that lasted until 1190 BCE—when Setnakht took the throne, founding the 20th dynasty.

Setnakht ruled for only a short time, from 1190 to 1187 BCE, and most of his reign was taken up with trying to restore order in a troubled kingdom. His son Ramses III (ruled 1187–1156 BCE) inherited a stable society and was the New Kingdom's last great pharaoh.

In this wall painting from the tomb of Tutankhamen, the pharaoh is welcomed into the land of the gods by the goddess Nut.

Although his kingdom was internally secure, Ramses III was harassed by continuing attempts at invasion by the Libyans and the Sea Peoples. Ramses successfully repulsed these invasions in a series of land and naval battles, but the military campaigns put a great strain on the Egyptian economy, and after Ramses' death, the kingdom began to decline.

The priests and the army

The reigns of the later Ramesside kings saw a major increase in the power of two groups—the priests and the army. The temples were major owners of land, and the priests profited from this, becoming virtually independent from the central bureaucracy. In particular, the temple of Amon at Karnak became so powerful that it practically controlled Upper Egypt. Because the office of priest was hereditary, the high priests became a dynasty to rival the royal dynasty.

To defend Egypt's borders, the pharaohs had built up a powerful standing army. This army was augmented by mercenaries, who were often prisoners of war who had agreed to fight for Egypt. These mercenaries were established in military colonies, and in time, they became a significant political force in the kingdom.

The increasing power of the army and the priests of Amon put an end to the New Kingdom around 1075 BCE. During a time of civil unrest in Thebes, the pharaoh sent Panehsi, the viceroy of Kush, to restore order. However, he was unsuccessful; Herihor, a new high priest of Amon, took control of the Theban region and claimed to be king, while the pharaoh looked on helplessly from his distant residence in the Nile Delta.

The Third Intermediate period

The Third Intermediate period (c. 1075–664 BCE) ran from the 21st dynasty to the 25th dynasty. The beginning of the

21st dynasty saw the country divided. The first king, Smendes, ruled from Tanis in the northeastern delta, while the Theban priests controlled the south. The pharaoh was represented in Thebes by one of his daughters, who assumed the title "Divine Wife of Amon." Thebes eventually became a separate state (the "Divine State of Amon") guided by the high priests and the wives of the god. As such, it continued to exist even after the

This colossal statue from the 13th century BCE depicts Ramses II, one of the greatest of the New Kingdom pharaohs.

WOMEN IN ANCIENT EGYPT

Women enjoyed a far higher status in ancient Egypt than in most other early societies. In many aspects, they were considered the equal of men; they had the right to own land, represent themselves in legal proceedings, and conduct a business.

Young girls remained at home with their mothers to receive training in domestic duties and household management. Unlike boys, girls were never sent to school, but they might be taught to read and write at home. Girls from peasant families were usually married when they were around 12 years old; girls from better-off families married a little later. Marriages were generally arranged, although the young people might have some say in the matter. Before a marriage took place in richer families, the couple signed a pre-nuptial agreement, which stipulated that the husband was to pay an allowance to his wife and that any material possessions she brought to the marriage would remain hers if the marriage ended.

For girls who did not marry, other opportunities were available. Some single women became singers, musicians, dancers, or acrobats. Others might find employment with a wealthy family as a maid or nanny, while a girl from a noble family could become a priestess.

For most women, daily work consisted of looking after the home and children. Wheat had to be ground into flour, which was then made into bread and baked in a clay oven. Other food, such as fish, meat, and vegetables, might be boiled or roasted over an open fire. A mother would generally weave flax into linen and then make clothes for her family—men generally wore a short skirt called a kilt and women wore a straight dress held up with straps.

Egyptians placed great emphasis on cleanliness, and both women and men would bathe daily, either in the river or in a basin of water in the house. They then anointed themselves with perfumed oil and applied face makeup.

The temple complex at Abu Simbel, carved out of the mountainside during the reign of Ramses II (ruled 1279–1213 BCE), is one of Egypt's most popular tourist attractions.

other parts of Egypt were defeated by other nations.

During the 21st dynasty, Libyan principalities arose in the Nile Delta, and in 950 BCE, a Libyan military leader named Sheshonk seized the throne, establishing the 22nd dynasty (950–730 BCE). While the Libyans consolidated their position in the north by establishing military garrisons, they attempted to improve relations with Thebes through political marriages with priestly families. Thebes continued to resent the northern dynasty, however, and eventually established the rival 23rd dynasty in the south.

The latter part of the 22nd dynasty was characterized by an increasing fragmentation of land and by power struggles. In 730 BCE, a Kushite ruler called Piye raided as far north as Memphis, and the northern rulers were forced to pay him tribute. However, after Piye returned to Kush, the Libyan prince Tefnakhte of Sais reassertd his claims in the north. His son Bocchoris succeeded him as the sole pharaoh of the 24th dynasty (c. 722–715 BCE). The Libyan domination was finally ended by Piye's brother Shabaka, who succeeded in bringing the whole of Egypt under his control and founded the 25th dynasty.

The Late period

Egypt remained under Nubian rule for almost 50 years, and it was a time of internal peace and prosperity. However, the might of Assyria had been growing since the ninth century, and in 671 BCE, the Assyrian king Esarhaddon invaded Egypt and took Memphis. For the next several years, campaigns were fought on Egyptian soil between Assyrians and Egyptian kings, but problems at home eventually forced the Assyrians to withdraw, leaving Psamtik I to inaugurate the 26th dynasty (664–525 BCE). Under Psamtik, north and south were united once more.

This hallway leads to the tomb of Ramses VI, who reigned in the 12th century BCE.

In 525 BCE, the Persians conquered Egypt, and the Persian king Cambyses became the first ruler of the 27th dynasty. The country remained under Persian domination until 404 BCE. Native Egyptian rulers then reasserted their independence through the next three dynasties. The 31st dynasty saw a return to Persian rule, which held until Alexander the Great conquered Egypt in 332 BCE, making it part of the Greek world.

See also:

The Assyrians (volume 2, page 208) • Egypt's Middle Kingdom (volume 1, page 78) • Egypt's Old Kingdom (volume 1, page 70) • The Hittites (volume 2, page 150) • The Persians (volume 2, page 232)

THE BABYLONIANS

TIME LINE

1894 BCE
Sumu-abu seizes power in Babylon, founding city's first dynasty.

c. 1792 BCE
Hammurabi ascends to throne of Babylon; carves out huge empire over course of next 42 years.

1595 BCE
Hittite king Mursilis I sacks Babylon; in symbolic act steals statue of Marduk from its temple.

1570 BCE
Kassite king Agum II captures Babylon; Kassite kings rule Babylon for next four and a half centuries.

605 BCE
Nebuchadnezzar II becomes king of Babylon; through series of military conquests, creates Neo-Babylonian Empire.

539 BCE
Babylon falls to Persians.

In the first and second millenniums BCE, the power and influence of the Mesopotamian city of Babylon fluctuated greatly. The periods of its greatest power came during the reigns of Hammurabi and Nebuchadnezzar II—more than a thousand years apart.

The fall of the third dynasty of Ur in 2004 BCE marked the start of a new period in Mesopotamian history—the Old Babylonian period, which lasted until the end of the first dynasty of Babylon in 1595 BCE. During this period, the Sumerian civilization declined, and Babylon became the political and cultural center of Mesopotamia.

In the first part of this period, semi-nomadic Amorite tribes from the western desert invaded the Mesopotamian plain and captured several cities. The ensuing battles between the invaders and the original inhabitants made this a time of great confusion. Eventually, two city-states came to prominence—Isin and Larsa. The victorious chiefs ruling the conquered cities established their own dynasties and, for the most part, assimilated the existing Sumerian culture.

The first dynasty of Babylon

Around 1894 BCE, an Amorite called Sumu-abu seized power in the Akkadian city of Babylon, founding the first dynasty of Babylon. At that time, Babylon was no more than a minor city in a highly unstable area, but over the next 100 years, the Babylonian kings consolidated their position, and when the sixth king of the dynasty, Hammurabi, came to the throne around 1792 BCE, he inherited a secure state with growing influence.

Hammurabi was an energetic young man with an outstanding gift for diplomacy and military strategy. During the 42 years of his reign, he transformed Babylon into the preeminent city of Mesopotamia and created an empire that extended from Assyria in the north to the Persian Gulf in the south. Arts and sciences flourished, making it the "golden age" of the Old Empire.

Initially, Hammurabi devoted himself to building temples and canals and establishing his code of law. For several years, he then concentrated on building cordial relations with neighboring rulers. In the 29th year of his reign, he switched tactics, changing to an aggressive policy of extending his empire by military means. In 1762 BCE, he conquered Larsa. He followed this by defeating the kings of Elam, Mari, and Eshnunna and two powerful kings in northern Mesopotamia, Shamshi-Adad I and Ishme-Dagan. He then annexed the whole of Sumer. In the north, he took control of Ashur and Nineveh, claiming the title "King of Sumer and Akkad."

Hammurabi's influence on the history of Mesopotamia was immense. Besides building a vast empire, he also made Babylon such an important Mesopotamian center that it remained the leading city of western Asia long after his death in 1750 BCE.

According to the sources that have survived, Hammurabi was a fair and just ruler. From a central government in the city of Babylon, he cared for his subjects and defended the weak, even the inhabitants of two cities he destroyed—Mari and Eshnunna. He treated the people who lived there leniently and built new homes for those who had lost their dwellings. He took a personal interest in the affairs of the empire, supervising such matters as irrigation and agriculture, tax collection, and the construction of many buildings, especially temples.

The Code of Hammurabi

One of Hammurabi's concerns was to ensure that the rule of law and justice was observed throughout his lands. To this end, he devised a collection of laws and edicts, which is now known as the Code of Hammurabi.

Although Ur-Nammu, king of Ur, had introduced what appears to be the first code of law in Mesopotamia some three centuries earlier, Hammurabi's code is the earliest known complete legal classification. Hammurabi claimed that his code was divinely inspired, but it

This relief of a bull, created in the sixth century BCE, once adorned the walls of Babylon. The Babylonians believed that bulls were sacred animals.

THE EMPIRE OF HAMMURABI

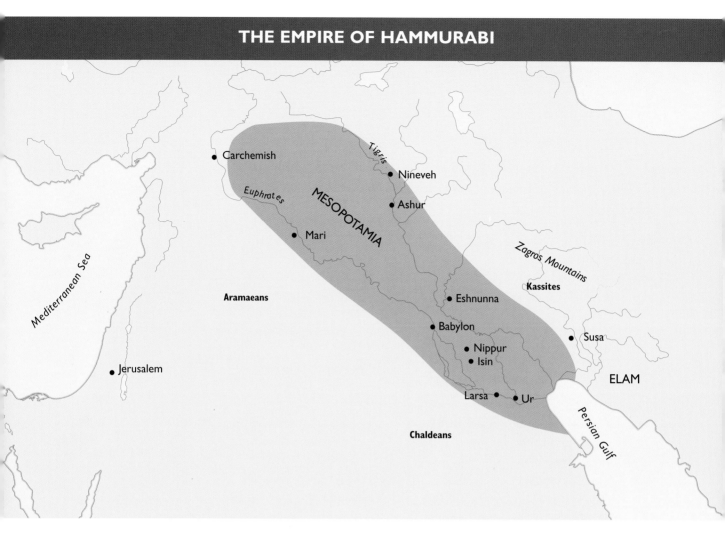

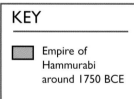

KEY

Empire of
Hammurabi
around 1750 BCE

has now been established that it was rooted in an ancient Mesopotamian legal tradition that dated back to the time of the Sumerians.

The code was discovered in the winter of 1901–1902 CE by a French archaeological expedition that was excavating the ruins of Susa in southwest Iran (ancient Elam). The team unearthed three pieces of stone, which had obviously once made up a single block, engraved in cuneiform script. When restored, the stone blocks formed a stele carved out of black diorite and standing 7 feet 4 inches (2.2 m) high. It appears that the stele was stolen from Babylon by a king of Elam in 1158 BCE.

At the top of the stele is a relief that shows the sun god Shamash (who was associated with justice) handing Hammurabi a staff and ring, the emblems of his power to administer the law. Below the relief are 16 horizontal columns of cuneiform text in Akkadian, the Semitic language spoken in Mesopotamia at that time. On the reverse side, there are 28 further columns of text. The code consists of a prologue, a middle section containing the laws, and an epilogue.

Prologue and procedures

Hammurabi's code opens with a prologue, in which Hammurabi suggests that the gods have given him a special role as lawgiver and protector of the weak: "Anum and Enlil appointed me to promote the well-being of the people, me, Hammurabi, the pious, god-fearing ruler! To insure that law would rule in the whole land, to destroy the wicked and the evil so that the strong do not oppress the weak, to rise as the sun above the people and to light the land, Hammurabi, the people's shepherd, the one named by Enlil, that am I."

The prologue is followed by the laws themselves, divided into 28 paragraphs. Modern commentators have identified 282 laws, including property laws, commercial laws, and laws relating to marriage. The penalties mentioned range from fines and beatings to mutilation (such as the cutting off of a hand or putting out of an eye) and death. The punishments of imprisonment and forced labor were unknown.

The first few laws deal with legal procedures and the penalties for not following them correctly. For example, one law states that if a free man accuses another free man of murder but cannot prove guilt, the accuser himself will be put to death. Another law decrees that if a free man bears witness in a case and cannot prove his statement, the witness himself will be executed, but only if the case involves a matter of life and death.

Theft laws and family laws

Several laws deal with breaches of contract, property rights, and slaves. Some of the punishments for theft and burglary were very specific. For example, if a free man made a hole in a house with an intent to steal from it, he would be executed in front of that hole and then bricked in. If, on the other hand, a fire broke out in the house of a free man, and another free man entered to extinguish the fire but instead stole some of the inhabitant's possessions, the thief would be thrown into the fire and burned alive.

No less than 70 articles in the code deal with family law. The family was the basic unit of society. Sons had greater rights than daughters, however. For

example, if only daughters were born to the parents, a son-in-law could take on all the functions of a son. It was acceptable to adopt a child, even though this practice was rare in other parts of the Semitic world. The adopted child might be an orphan or the child of a concubine or of relatives or friends.

Several other laws dealt with marriage (see box, page 118) and relations between the sexes. A sexual transgression could be harshly punished. If the wife of a free man was caught having sex with another man, both would be tied up, thrown into the Euphrates River, and left to drown.

Law and rank

The laws contained in Hammurabi's code did not apply equally to everyone. In Babylonian society, the people occupied different ranks, and their rights were determined by their status. At the top were the free people of the *awilu* class. These were the aristocrats, the wealthy, and the property owners, who probably lived in

The stele of King Hammurabi, from the 18th century BCE, is inscribed with his legal code, the first such code to survive in its entirety.

MARI

Mari was an ancient Semitic kingdom located on the upper Euphrates River in Syria at the intersection of a number of trade routes. As a pivotal center of trade, Mari had two eras of greatness, one during the first half of the third millennium BCE and another in the early part of the second millennium BCE. Its prosperity made it a rival to the Akkadian Empire of Sargon and the Babylonian Empire of Hammurabi. It was subdued by both of those powerful states.

The remains of Mari were discovered in 1933 CE by the French archaeologist André Parrot, who was excavating near Tell Hariri in Syria, close to the Iraqi border. His finds showed that the city had two golden ages. The first was ended when it was conquered by Sargon of Akkad, after which it was ruled first by Akkad, then by Ur, and finally by the emerging Ashur. It then had a short period of independence under its own dynasty; Zimrilim (ruled 1779–1757 BCE) was its most famous king. For a while, Zimrilim was an ally of Hammurabi. The kings exchanged cordial letters and sent ambassadors to each other's court. However, after conquering Larsa, Hammurabi turned on Mari around 1757 BCE, annexing it and destroying Zimrilim's capital city and palace.

The archaeological finds from the first period were sensational. A palace, a ziggurat, and a series of small temples, most of which were devoted to Semitic gods and goddesses, dated from that period. Two especially noteworthy temples were dedicated to Ishtar and Dagan. The style of the statues shows a marked Sumerian influence, suggesting that Mari had close contact with southern Mesopotamia at that time.

The palace of Zimrilim, dating from the second period, was a magnificent structure that must have been the envy of many contemporary kings. With more than 300 rooms, it measured 600 by 410 feet (183 by 125 m). The palace's rooms included royal apartments, offices, and storerooms. The throne room was painted with striking murals, one of which showed Zimrilim being anointed as king by the goddess Ishtar.

This wall painting from a palace at Mari shows a sacrificial scene.

two-story brick houses with several rooms, in which the walls might be plastered. Next came a middle class of free people, called the *mushkenu*, who probably lived in smaller, single-story houses of mud brick.

At the bottom of the social hierarchy were the slaves, or *wardu*, who lived in poorer quarters. Most slaves were prisoners of war and were used by the king on public works programs, such as the construction of temples, roads, and irrigation canals. Others were people who had once been free but had been made slaves as the legal penalty for infractions of Hammurabi's code. Some slaves had been sold into slavery by their parents.

Slaves were considered to be property that could be bought and sold or used to pay debts. Under the code, whole families could be handed over to a creditor as slaves,

but only for a maximum of three years. Slaves were generally well treated (largely for economic reasons), and they also had some rights under the law. They were permitted to conduct business and even to borrow money and purchase their freedom.

Within this class structure, crime carried different penalties according to who had committed it and whom it was committed against. If a free man broke the leg of a nobleman, then his own leg would be broken as punishment. If he committed the same crime against a fellow member of the

This Babylonian statue from the 18th century BCE depicts a praying man. It is possible that the statue depicts King Hammurabi himself.

THE MARI LETTERS

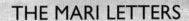

When Mari was excavated in 1933 CE, an archive containing some 25,000 clay tablets was uncovered. The Mari Letters are made up of correspondence exchanged between the rulers of Mari and other kings and chieftains. As such, they provide a wealth of fascinating detail on the life of people in the central Euphrates region around 1800 BCE.

For example, a general wrote to the palace to complain that the auxiliaries he was expecting from the local communities were not forthcoming. He suggested that a criminal should be taken from prison and executed and that the criminal's head should be carried around the reluctant encampments, "so the soldiers will become afraid and will assemble here quickly."

Another letter from a son to his mother complained that he had only ragged clothes to wear even though "the clothes of young men are becoming more and more beautiful here.... [And even though the son of] a servant of my father has two new sets of clothes, you are already objecting to one new set for me!"

When Shamshi-Adad I (ruled 1813–1781 BCE) of Assyria was overlord of Mari, he appointed his son Yasmah-Adad as his viceroy there. However, the arrangement appears to have been far from satisfactory, and in a series of bitter letters, the father upbraids the son for his shortcomings, comparing him unfavorably with his more capable elder brother, who was a general of an army.

This depiction of people bringing goods as tribute is from Hammurabi's stele, which was created in the 18th century BCE.

middle class, the punishment would only be a fine of one silver mina. If he broke the leg of a slave, however, he would have to pay the slave's owner half of the slave's value in compensation.

Trade laws

There were various penalties for damage caused by neglect in various trades. For example, an architect who built a house that collapsed and killed the owner would be executed. Subsequent articles laid down the fixed rates payable for services rendered by trades. Workers in these trades were entitled to a minimum wage and to three days off each month. The code also laid down the maximum interest that could be charged for debt— not more than 33 percent was permitted for private debts.

Epilogue to the code

The code closes with an epilogue in praise of Hammurabi, who had been called by the gods to allow "the land to enjoy stable government and good rule." He wrote the laws on stone, he stated, so that "the strong may not oppress the weak, and that justice may be dealt to the orphan and the widow." He went on to say that he had inscribed his precious words on a stele and established it in Babylon before the statue of himself called the "King of Justice."

The epilogue ends with these words: "Let any oppressed man who has a cause come into the presence of my statue as king of justice, and let him have the inscription on my stele read out to him. Let him hear my precious words, so that my stele may make his rights clear to him, and let him know the law that applies to him, so that his heart may be set at ease."

Inherited gods

The gods of Babylonia were inherited from the Sumerians and Akkadians. The original head of this pantheon had been the deity Anu, god of the sky, but by the Babylonian period, his son, the god Enlil, the "Lord of the Winds," was considered to be the king of the gods. One of the most important female deities was Ishtar, the goddess of love and war. Known to the Sumerians as Inanna, she was identified with Venus, the evening star, and was often shown riding a lion, her sacred animal. From the Akkadians, the Babylonians adopted two other important gods—Shamash (the sun god) and Sin (the moon god). Two other deities of particular significance were the grain god Dagan and the weather god Adad, who was responsible for bringing rain.

Shamash had a particularly important role as the great judge, the "destroyer of evil" who watched over the Babylonians like a shepherd over his flock. He was thought to travel the skies daily in his chariot, seeing everything that happened on earth.

Creation and afterlife

One god who came to particular prominence during the reign of Hammurabi was Marduk. Marduk was important because of the role that he played in the Babylonian story of creation, which was told in an epic poem known as the *Enuma Elish*. The poem relates how Marduk defeated Tiamat, a primeval sea monster that was a symbol of chaos. From the body of this monster, Marduk made the earth and the heavens. The idea of a creator god creating order out of chaos was common in ancient societies. Marduk's victory over Tiamat was commemorated at every celebration of the Babylonian New Year and the *Enuma Elish* was recited at the festivals.

The Babylonians apparently believed in an afterlife. The souls of the dead were thought to journey to a netherworld and to continue life there in much the same way as on earth. For this reason, the dead were buried with the same tools, weapons, clothes, and jewelry that they had used on earth.

Another central aspect of Babylonian religion was the relationship of the gods

This relief depicts a musician playing a harp and dates to the early second millennium BCE.

These ancient stone walls are the remains of Hammurabi's palace in Babylon.

Much of the Code of Hammurabi consists of laws dating back to ancient times, so the sections dealing with marriage often describe rules that had been in force in Mesopotamia for centuries. Family law allowed a man to have several wives, but he was only bound to one.

After the bride's parents had consented to the union, the marriage took place in a ceremony that consisted simply of witnessing the marriage contract. This agreement was inscribed on a clay tablet and defined the position of the two parties. The husband listed his conditions for accepting the woman as his wife, while the contract also contained a description of the woman's rights and duties. It spelled out the amount of money she would receive if she were to be rejected in the future and her punishment if she were to be unfaithful.

The marriage was also marked by the transfer of money or property from the bridegroom to his future father-in-law. After the marriage ceremony, these assets remained the possession of the bride's father. He in turn had to make a payment of a dowry, which remained the property of the wife. If the marriage was not completed because of a fault on the part of the groom, the bride's father would keep the money he had received. However, if the bride or her family defaulted so that the wedding did not take place, they had to pay back double the money they had received.

Under the old Sumerian law, a wife had various legal rights. She could be a witness to a contract; she could own property and administer it without reference to her husband; and she could engage independently in business. She was also entitled to the income from any assets she received from her husband. However, her husband could divorce her on very slender grounds, whereas it was much more difficult for her to divorce her husband..

in heaven with their representations on earth—their statues in the temples. The deity was thought to be present in his statue, so the statues were clothed, fed daily, and addressed as if they were living beings. The Babylonians believed they had been put on earth in order to serve the gods. For this reason, it was vitally important that they discovered the will of the gods.

Divination and astronomy

Various means were used to establish the thoughts of the gods. The priests who carried out such divination rituals were important people and were consulted by both high officials and ordinary citizens. The priests used a variety of means to determine the will of the gods, including studying the behavior of animals within the temple enclosure, observing the patterns of oil in water or smoke from incense, and studying the movements of heavenly bodies. Another type of divination involved the study of the internal organs of sacrificial animals; clay models of sheep livers bearing all kinds of inscriptions have been found in Mesopotamia.

Because the study of heavenly bodies was an important source of omens, a network of observatories was set up to study the stars and phenomena such as lightning, earthquakes, thunderstorms, and hail. These observatories collected astronomical data that is astonishingly accurate; the Babylonians have justly been called the fathers of astronomy.

This statue depicts King Ishtupilum, who was a ruler of Mari in the 18th century BCE. Mari was a powerful city-state that was a rival of Babylon.

The study of mathematics

The Babylonians developed a remarkably advanced mathematical system, based on the sexagesimal system of numbers (which uses sixty as a base number) that they had inherited from the Sumerians. Evidence collected from tablets intended for school use shows that they had multiplication and division tables, as well as tables for working out squares and square roots.

It is clear that Babylonian students of mathematics were taught how to solve geometric and algebraic problems and that much of the study was directed toward practical problems associated with engineering and quantity surveying. The Babylonians had standardized measures for weight, volume, length, and area, and their cuneiform writing had special combinations of signs to represent numbers, enabling elaborate calculations to be carried out.

Medicine

Ancient Babylonian texts indicate that doctors used various means to establish the cause of a patient's illness and the likelihood of recovery. The study of omens was an important part of the doctor's job; for example, the appearance of a particular type of animal in the vicinity of the patient was believed to indicate whether he or she would recover.

However, doctors also had more practical skills. They prescribed herbal remedies for specific illnesses and also sometimes carried out surgical operations. Mesopotamian doctors were skillful in setting broken bones. Surgery could be dangerous for both doctor and patient, however; doctors who accidentally injured people during surgical operations faced harsh punishments.

Fall of an empire

After the death of Hammurabi, the Babylonian Empire came under attack. Hammurabi's son Samsu-ilina (ruled 1749–1712 BCE) had to cope with rebellious cities in the south, while the Kassites from the east began making incursions into the weakening empire. By the end of Samsu-ilina's reign, the so-called Sealand dynasty was in control of southern Mesopotamia from the Persian Gulf to Nippur. For the next 100 years or so, Babylonia continued to lose both land and prestige to these enemy states. Around 1595 BCE, the Hittite king Mursilis I raided Babylon, sacking the city and seizing its wealth. In a symbolic act, he stole the statue of Marduk from the god's temple in the center of Babylon. The sacking of Babylon marked the end of Hammurabi's dynasty.

The next stage of Babylon's history is shrouded in mystery. It seems that the ruined state of Babylon was easy prey for its next conquerors, the kings of the Sealand dynasty, who controlled the city for a time. Then, around 1570 BCE, a Kassite king called Agum II seized power in Babylonia, soon controlling the area from the Euphrates to the Zagros Mountains. He is said to have recaptured the statue of Marduk and restored it to its temple, decking it out in a new set of clothes. This act would have made him popular with the Babylonians, and as the Kassite kings were also willing to adopt the customs, religion, and even the language of the conquered land, they soon became almost indistinguishable from earlier Mesopotamian rulers.

Kassite rule

The Kassite kings ruled Babylonia for the next four and a half centuries, during which time the city of Babylon once again became the administrative and cultural capital of a substantial Mesopotamian empire.

However, although the Kassites were successful in retaining power for a long time, they were constantly threatened by aggressive states menacing their borders. To the east, the Hurrians, who hailed from northwest Iran, were establishing a number of small states, while in the north, the kingdom of the Mittani was growing ever more powerful.

In the early 13th century BCE, the Kassites entered into a treaty of friendship with the Hittites. The pact was supposed to act as some kind of insurance against the growing might of Assyria. However, in 1225 BCE, Babylon was attacked and sacked by the Assyrian king Tukulti-Ninurta I, who massacred the city's inhabitants. Marduk's statue was

This piece of Assyrian metalwork from the eighth century BCE depicts a worshipper before the goddess Ishtar. Ishtar was worshipped by both the Babylonians and the Assyrians.

again carried off, this time to Assyria. This sacrilege was too much for the Babylonians, and even for some Assyrians, and in 1197 BCE, Tukulti-Ninurta was assassinated. The Kassite Babylonians regained their independence for a while, but in 1158 BCE, the Elamite king Shutruk-Nahhunte I sacked Babylon, deposed its king, and put an end to the Kassite dynasty.

The Second Dynasty of Isin

After a period of instability, a new royal line centered on the city of Isin emerged. This line was called the Second Dynasty of Isin, and its most famous king was Nebuchadnezzar I, who reigned from around 1125 to 1104 BCE. Nebuchadnezzar restored the morale of the Babylonians by inflicting a crushing defeat on the Elamites. Leading an army across the desert, he confronted the enemy before their capital, Susa. After his victory, he recovered the statue of Marduk, which Shutruk-Nahhunte had taken to Susa after the sack of Babylon.

During the next few centuries, Babylon was ruled by a succession of minor dynasties. This period was marked by numerous incursions of Aramaean tribesmen from the west who seized farming land wherever they could. Eventually, the Aramaeans managed to establish themselves permanently in the south, where they adapted to the local culture and became a major part of the population. However, the empire suffered from their plundering raids and many of the original Babylonians began to suffer from famine and poverty.

The New Empire

During the tenth and ninth centuries BCE, the Babylonians and Assyrians managed to coexist without too much friction, but in the eighth century BCE, a new foe appeared to disturb the political scene. The Chaldeans, a tribe of Semitic speakers, settled around the Persian Gulf. Unlike the seminomadic Aramaeans, the Chaldeans lived in prosperous villages, keeping cattle and horses and controlling the trade routes to the east. The Chaldean chiefs aspired to the Babylonian throne, and during the eighth century BCE, a Chaldean general

When rolled in wet clay, the Babylonian cylinder seal on the left would have created an imprint similar to that on the right. This particular seal, made in the 16th century BCE, depicts someone making an offering to a deity.

This reconstruction of Babylon's Ishtar Gate, made partially from the original tiles, stands in Berlin's Pergamon Museum. The original was constructed in the sixth century BCE.

named Merodach-baladan succeeded twice in briefly seizing the crown of Babylonia.

Defeat of the Assyrians

In 729 BCE, following the death of the Babylonian ruler Nabu-nasir, the Assyrian king Tiglath-pileser III led a campaign into Babylonia. After a series of military victories, he managed to establish Assyrian ascendancy over the region and make himself king of Babylonia. The Assyrians remained overlords of Babylon until 626 BCE, when a Chaldean general called Napolassar led a campaign of determined onslaughts aimed at ousting the Assyrians from the Babylonian plain.

Napolassar successfully managed to drive the Assyrians out. He then took the Babylonian crown for himself, restoring Babylonian independence from Assyria and ushering in the greatest period of Babylonian history.

The power of Assyria was on the wane, and Napolassar followed up his victory at home by joining forces with the Medes from the Iranian plain and attacking the Assyrians from two sides. Nineveh, the Assyrian capital, was taken in 612 BCE; three years later, the Assyrian Empire was totally destroyed. By this victory, Napolassar became king of a vast empire that stretched from the Mediterranean Sea to the Persian Gulf.

THE EPIC OF GILGAMESH

Many works of literature have survived from Babylonian times, the most famous of which is the *Epic of Gilgamesh*. This epic, inscribed in Akkadian cuneiform, was found on clay tablets among the remains of the library of the Assyrian king Ashurbanipal (ruled 668–627 BCE) when his capital, Nineveh, was being excavated in the 19th century CE. This epic dates from the time of Hammurabi and tells the story of Gilgamesh, a legendary king of Sumer whose character may have been based on that of one of the early rulers of Uruk.

As befits a legendary hero, Gilgamesh is immensely tall—11 feet (3.35 m)—and is two-thirds god and one-third human. He is described as striding "through the streets of Uruk like a wild ox, sublime of gait." Gilgamesh acquires a companion, a wild hairy man called Enkidu, who has proved the king's equal in a wrestling match. Together, the two heroes go forth into the world to perform great deeds. Their first adventure involves a trip to the forests of Lebanon, where they defeat the fearsome giant Chumbaba, king of the Cedar Mountain.

After more adventures, Enkidu falls ill and dies. Gilgamesh is heartbroken, and from then on, the story is no longer about an invincible hero and his glorious deeds; it is about a desperate, only-too-human Gilgamesh engaged in a bitter fight with death, the only enemy he cannot escape. Setting out on a search for immortality, Gilgamesh journeys to the "island of the blessed," where he eventually finds the herb of life deep in a spring. He picks the herb and starts on his return journey. Along the way, however, he goes swimming in a lake, leaving the precious herb of life on the shore, where it is eaten by a snake.

Robbed of his chance at immortality, Gilgamesh must settle for being mortal. However, he finds solace in contemplating his life's work. He built the walls of the great city of Uruk, and these walls are so strong that he predicts they will last for all eternity. So far, he has not been proved wrong.

This Assyrian relief sculpture from the eighth century BCE is believed to depict the hero Gilgamesh.

THE CITY OF BABYLON

The ancient city of Babylon lies on the Euphrates River in present-day Iraq, around 56 miles (90 km) south of Baghdad. Babylon was excavated between 1899 and 1913 CE by a German archaeological team led by Robert Koldewey, who uncovered the city as it had been in its final years, in the reign of Nebuchadnezzar II. The city was built on either side of the Euphrates, which flowed though its middle. Babylon covered an area of 2,100 acres (850 ha) and was home to a quarter of a million people, making it larger than many modern towns.

Babylon was rectangular in shape and was surrounded by two mighty walls. These walls were so thick that, according to the Greek historian Herodotus, it was possible for two chariots to be driven side by side along the top of each wall. The walls were pierced by nine great gates made of bronze. The most magnificent of them was the Ishtar Gate, which was covered with yellow and blue tiles that incorporated reliefs of lions and bulls, symbols of the gods Ishtar and Adad. Reconstructions of this gate can be seen in Baghdad and Berlin.

Inside the city walls were the palace of Nebuchadnezzar, the Esagila (the main temple of Marduk, the patron god of Babylon), and houses for the citizens. The temple was connected to the Ishtar Gate by a wide avenue called the Processional Way. During the annual New Year festivities, the king led a procession in which the statue of Marduk was carried through the Ishtar Gate to temples outside the city. North of Marduk's temple stood the ziggurat of Babylon, called the Etemenanki or "House of the Foundation of Heaven and Earth." It had seven stories and rose to a height of 300 feet (91 m). Many commentators have identified this ziggurat with the Tower of Babel in the Bible.

Nebuchadnezzar II

The taking of Nineveh marked the beginning of the Neo-Babylonian Empire. In 605 BCE, Napolassar's son Nebuchadnezzar led a campaign against the Egyptians, who had marched into Syria as far as Carchemish on the upper Euphrates River. He achieved a magnificent victory, but on the same day, he received news of his father's death. Hurrying back to Babylon, he ascended the throne as Nebuchadnezzar II, beginning one of the most brilliant reigns in the history of Babylon.

Nebuchadnezzar followed up his triumph at Carchemish by conquering Syria, Phoenicia, and Judah, where Jerusalem fell to him in 597 BCE. Several years later, Jerusalem rebelled, but after a siege, the Babylonians took it again.

Nebuchadnezzar exacted a terrible revenge on the inhabitants of Jerusalem. The rebellious governor was forced to watch while his sons were killed in front of him. He was then blinded and taken in chains to Babylon. Jerusalem was put to the torch, its leaders were executed, and most of its inhabitants were deported to Babylonia. Because of his destruction of Jerusalem, Nebuchadnezzar is a key figure in the Old Testament of the Bible, where his exploits are described in the Book of Daniel.

The Hanging Gardens

Nebuchadnezzar is chiefly remembered today for inaugurating a great building program in Babylon. Attempting to rebuild the empire of Hammurabi, he restored old temples and constructed new buildings throughout Babylonia. He rebuilt Babylon, enlarging it and making it far more splendid than it had ever been. He also embellished it with the famous Hanging Gardens, one of the seven wonders of the world. The gardens were reputedly built as a gift for his wife, a Median princess named Amyitis, so she would not miss the landscape of her homeland. The Hanging Gardens were famous in the ancient world and were mentioned in the works of several later Greek writers, including Strabo and Diodorus Siculus. However, present-day archaeological excavations have been unable to locate them.

After Nebuchadnezzar's death in 562 BCE, revival efforts were lost in a series of power struggles. In 556 BCE, an elderly general named Nabonidus took the throne. He is a mysterious figure. Only three years into his reign, he left Babylon in the care of his son Belshazzar and went to live in Teiman in the Arabian Desert. Ten years later, he returned to Babylon, but his reign was doomed. In 539 BCE, Cyrus, king of Persia, invaded Babylonia. Nabonidus fled, but he and his son were both captured and killed. The Persians captured Babylon without resistance. Babylonia was annexed, becoming a province of the Persian Empire. Its days as an independent realm were at an end.

See also:

The Assyrians (volume 2, page 208) • The Hittites (volume 2, page 150) • The Persians (volume 2, page 232) • The Sumerians (volume 1, page 54)

The Hanging Gardens of Babylon, depicted here in an 18th-century-CE engraving, are believed to have been built by King Nebuchadnezzar II to ease the homesickness of his bride.

TIME LINE

	WESTERN ASIA, EUROPE, AND THE MEDITERRANEAN		REST OF THE WORLD	
	c. 2 million BCE	Early humans begin to make stone tools.	**c. 2 million BCE**	*Homo habilis* and *Homo erectus* evolve.
	c. 30,000 BCE	Earliest cave paintings created.	**c. 30,000 BCE**	Lapita culture develops in New Guinea.
	c. 24,000 BCE	Figurine known as Venus of Willendorf carved in central Europe (modern Austria).		
c. 10,000 BCE	**c. 10,000 BCE**	First permanent settlements established in western Asia by people of Natufian culture.	**c. 10,000 BCE**	End of Ice Age; land bridge between Alaska and Siberia submerged by Bering Strait.
	c. 8500 BCE	First farmers cultivate oats and barley in Syria; Neolithic period begins.	**c. 7500 BCE**	Jomon period, marked by distinctive pottery, begins in Japan.
	c. 7000 BCE	Craftsmen in Iran and Turkey begin making jewelry from copper and gold.		
	c. 6000 BCE	First European farming settlements established in Crete and Greece.	**c. 6000 BCE**	First farmers in southern Asia.
	c. 5000 BCE	Semitic-speaking people move into southern Mesopotamia.	**c. 5000 BCE**	Emergence of Yang-shao culture in China.
	c. 4000 BCE	Funnel-beaker culture flourishes in central Europe.	**c. 4500 BCE**	Inhabitants of Ukraine begin to domesticate horses.
	c. 3500 BCE	Bronze Age begins in the Caucasus.	**c. 3500 BCE**	Llamas domesticated in Peru.

	WESTERN ASIA, EUROPE, AND THE MEDITERRANEAN		REST OF THE WORLD	
	c. 3400 BCE	Sumerian culture emerges.		
	c. 3100 BCE	Work begins on ritual circle at Stonehenge, England.	c. 3100 BCE	Bronze Age reaches China.
c. 3000 BCE	c. 3000 BCE	Phoenicians begin to settle in region that is now Syria, Lebanon, and Israel. First settlement appears at Troy. People living in Aegean begin to make bronze; dawn of Minoan culture on Crete.	c. 3000 BCE	Earliest known American pottery produced in Ecuador and Colombia.
	c. 2900 BCE	Single-grave people replace funnel-beaker people in northern Europe.		
	c. 2800 BCE	Invaders with knowledge of metalwork arrive in Greek mainland.	c. 2700 BCE	Silk production begins in China.
	c. 2650 BCE	Old Kingdom begins in Egypt.		
	c. 2625 BCE	Step Pyramid constructed at Saqqara, Egypt.		
	c. 2600 BCE	Early Helladic II period begins in Greece.	c. 2600 BCE	Earliest Indus Valley civilization develops; inhabitants of present-day Peru begin to mummify their dead.
	c. 2550 BCE	Work begins on Great Pyramid of Giza.		
	c. 2500 BCE	Stone circle built at Avebury, England.	c. 2500 BCE	Pottery is made in Savannah River valley in North America.
	c. 2335 BCE	Sargon the Great founds Akkadian Empire, builds city of Akkad, and unites Mesopotamia under one ruler.	c. 2200 BCE	Establishment of first Chinese dynasty, the Xia.

	WESTERN ASIA, EUROPE, AND THE MEDITERRANEAN		REST OF THE WORLD	
	c. 2150 BCE	Akkadian Empire ends. In Egypt, Old Kingdom comes to end as power of pharaoh diminishes; First Intermediate period begins.		
	2112 BCE	Ascent of Ur-Nammu marks beginning of third dynasty of Ur.	c. 2100 BCE	People of the Ban Chiang culture in Thailand begin to make bronze artifacts.
	c. 2047 BCE	Mentuhotep II reunites Egypt; period known as Middle Kingdom dates from this event.		
	2004 BCE	Elamites sack Ur; end of Sumerian period.		
c. 2000 BCE	c. 2000 BCE	Indo-European peoples arrive in Greece from central Asia. Distinct Assyrian culture emerges in northern Mesopotamia.	c. 2000 BCE	Bronze Age begins in northern Africa. Rice cultivated by Phung Nguyen culture in northern Vietnam. Long-shan culture evolves in Yellow River Valley in China.
	1962 BCE	Sesostris I becomes king of Egypt.		
	c. 1900 BCE	Metalworkers in British Isles begin using bronze.		
	1894 BCE	Sumu-abu seizes power in Babylon, founding city's first dynasty.	c. 1850 BCE	Long-shan period comes to end in China.
	c. 1800 BCE	Unetician culture reaches height of influence in central Europe.	c. 1800 BCE	India's great Indus Valley cultures start to decline.
	c. 1792 BCE	Hammurabi ascends to throne of Babylon; carves out huge empire over course of next 42 years.	c. 1766 BCE	Shang dynasty begins rule of Yellow River Valley in China.

WESTERN ASIA, EUROPE, AND THE MEDITERRANEAN		REST OF THE WORLD	
c. 1700 BCE	Hittites begin using iron for weapons and tools.		
c. 1630 BCE	Asiatic Hyksos kings take control in northern Egypt; Second Intermediate period begins.		
c. 1600 BCE	Mycenae becomes major power on Greek mainland.	**c. 1600 BCE**	Poverty Point culture established in present-day Louisiana.
1595 BCE	Hittite king Mursilis I sacks Babylon and steals statue of Marduk from its temple.		
1570 BCE	Kassites capture Babylon, which they rule for next four and a half centuries.		
1550 BCE	Ascent of Ahmose to throne of Egypt marks beginning of New Kingdom.		
c. 1500 BCE	Tumulus culture replaces Unetician culture in parts of Europe.	**c. 1500 BCE**	Aryans enter India from central Asia; first Vedas composed. Preclassical period of Mayan culture begins. Olmec civilization emerges on coast of Gulf of Mexico.
1492 BCE	Thutmose I becomes first Egyptian ruler to be buried in Valley of the Kings.		
c. 1450 BCE	Minoan civilization comes to end. Palaces burned down.	**1384 BCE**	China's Shang dynasty establishes capital at Yin (present-day Anyang).
1353 BCE	Amenhotep IV becomes pharaoh in Egypt; introduces new religion based around worship of sun god.		

c. 1500 BCE (left margin marker)

WESTERN ASIA, EUROPE, AND THE MEDITERRANEAN		REST OF THE WORLD	
c. 1250 BCE	Mycenaean era comes to end, possibly as result of invasion from the north. Troy VIIa, the Troy of Homer, destroyed.	**c. 1250 BCE**	Olmec center established at San Lorenzo.
c. 1200 BCE	Hallstatt culture emerges in present-day Austria.	**c. 1200 BCE**	Orally transmitted Vedas first written down.
c. 1100 BCE	Phoenicia becomes dominant maritime power in Mediterranean. Greece enters Dark Age.	**c. 1100 BCE**	Iron Age begins in India.
c. 1075 BCE	New Kingdom ends as Egypt splits into northern and southern states.		
c. 1050 BCE	Troy VIIb destroyed; city abandoned for centuries.	**c. 1050 BCE**	Shang dynasty in China ousted by Zhou.
c. 1000 BCE	King David makes Jerusalem capital of Kingdom of Israel.	**c. 1000 BCE**	Caste system emerges in India. Copper industry flourishes in southern Congo. Lapita culture reaches Fiji. Nubia gains independence from Egypt.
c. 950 BCE	Dorian invaders settle on Eurotas Plain; over next two centuries, they form city-state of Sparta.		
c. 900 BCE	Etruscan civilization develops in central Italy.	**c. 900 BCE**	First Brahmanas (Hindu sacred texts) composed. Small tribal kingdoms, known as *janapadas*, develop on Gangetic Plain.
c. 883 BCE	Ashurnasirpal II begins campaigns expanding Assyrian territory.		
c. 850 BCE	Greeks begin migrations to Cyprus, Crete, Aegean islands, and Anatolia.		
842 BCE	Most Phoenician ports in Levant are absorbed into Assyrian Empire.		

c. 1000 BCE

	WESTERN ASIA, EUROPE, AND THE MEDITERRANEAN		REST OF THE WORLD	
	814 BCE	Exiles from Tyre establish colony of Carthage.		
	c. 800 BCE	Poet Homer believed to have written *Iliad* and *Odyssey* around this time.	**c. 800 BCE**	Early Upanishads appended to Vedas.
	753 BCE	Traditional date given for founding of Rome.		
	c. 722 BCE	Northern Kingdom of Israel conquered by Assyrians.		
	c. 700 BCE	City of Byzantium founded. Scythians migrate into southern Russia from homeland in central Asia. Iron Age begins in Egypt.		
	c. 612 BCE	Nineveh falls to Babylonians; Assyrian Empire comes to end three years later.		
	c. 600 BCE	Iron Age arrives in northern Europe.	**c. 600 BCE**	First settlements occur at Teotihuacán in Mexico.
	c. 586 BCE	Jerusalem captured by Babylonians.		
	559 BCE	Cyrus the Great ascends Persian throne; later conquers Medes to absorb lands into Persian Empire.	**c. 563 BCE**	Siddharta Gautama (later known as the Buddha) born.
	539 BCE	Babylon falls to Persians.		
c. 500 BCE	**c. 500 BCE**	La Tène culture emerges in Switzerland.	**c. 500 BCE**	Zapotec people become powerful in Mexico. Magadha becomes leading state in India. Dong Son culture emerges in Vietnam.
	c. 450 BCE	Iberians learn art of producing iron.		

GLOSSARY

Akhetaton city built by the Egyptian pharaoh Akhenaton to replace the old Egyptian capital at Thebes; modern Amarna, Egypt.

Akkadians Semitic people who flourished in the third millennium BCE; named after Akkad, the capital of their empire.

Amarna Letters archive of clay tablets written in Babylonian cuneiform script; found at Akhetaton.

Amorites Semitic people who invaded Mesopotamia from the north and northwest beginning around 2000 BCE.

Anubis ancient Egyptian god of the dead; depicted as a jackal or as a man with the head of a jackal.

Aramaeans Semitic people who invaded southern Mesopotamia around 1100 BCE.

Aryans prehistoric inhabitants of Iran and northern India.

Assyrians people of northern Mesopotamia whose independent state, established in the 14th century BCE, became a major power in the region.

Aton Egyptian sun god Re when worshipped in the form of the disk of the sun.

Australopithecus "southern ape"; upright-walking hominid from around 4 million years ago; found in Africa.

ba in ancient Egyptian religion, one of the three main aspects of the soul, along with ka (the sum of a person's physical and intellectual qualities) and akh (the spirit in the hereafter).

Babylon major city in southern Mesopotamia. From 612 to 539 BCE, Babylon was the capital of the Neo-Babylonian Empire.

bell-beaker people Neolithic people who spread from Spain to northern Africa and western and central Europe between 2600 and 2000 BCE.

bronze copper-tin alloy widely used by 1700 BCE.

Bronze Age period during which bronze became the most important basic material; began around 3500 BCE in western Asia and around 1900 BCE in Europe.

cartouche oval frame enclosing the hieroglyphs of the name of an Egyptian sovereign.

Celts name given to a group of people occupying central and western Europe by 1000 BCE.

Chalcolithic period time when copper first began to be used to make tools and weapons, prior to the Bronze Age.

Chaldeans Aramaean people from southern Mesopotamia who caused the fall of Assyria in the seventh century BCE.

copper reddish brown metallic element; chemical symbol Cu.

cuneiform writing system with wedge-shaped characters that emerged at the end of the fourth millennium BCE. Cuneiform writing was used by the Sumerians and other early civilizations of western Asia.

cuprite mineral composed of copper oxide (chemical formula CuO); minor ore of the metal copper.

dolmen Neolithic burial chamber constructed from two or more great stone slabs set edgewise in the earth and a flat stone roof.

Dorians people from Macedonia and northern Greece who raided Egypt and neighboring areas in the 13th century BCE.

Early Dynastic period era of Egyptian history, also known as the Archaic period, when the pharaohs developed an effective system of ruling the whole of Egypt; lasted from around 2925 to 2650 BCE.

earthenware vessels and containers made of baked clay; in widespread use for cooking and storage by Neolithic cultures.

Elam ancient country in western Asia, roughly equivalent to modern southwestern Iran.

ensi governor of a Sumerian city-state; temple king and ruler of the city on behalf of the deity and the temple.

Epic of Gilgamesh ancient poem written in the Akkadian language. The earliest surviving written version was inscribed in cuneiform script in the seventh century BCE.

Euphrates river of western Asia that flows from the mountains of western Asia to the Persian Gulf. Its lower reaches form the western edge of Mesopotamia.

flint hard type of stone found in calcium and chalk layers; easily chipped to make tools; widely used in the Paleolithic and Mesolithic ages.

funnel-beaker culture culture that flourished around 2500 BCE in northern and central Europe; named for the characteristic shape of its earthenware.

Germanic tribes people from northwestern Europe who migrated southward, beginning around 200 BCE.

Gutians Iranian mountain people who invaded the Akkadian Empire repeatedly between around 2230 and 2100 BCE.

Hallstatt culture central European culture of the late Bronze and early Iron ages; flourished around 800 to 500 BCE.

hand-ax Paleolithic tool originally made of flint. Increasingly made of other stones, it was refined throughout the Paleolithic period.

Heliopolis city of ancient Egypt and site of a great temple to the sun god Re.

hieroglyphics writing system found in inscriptions on Egyptian monuments that uses characters in the form of pictures.

Hittites people who established an empire in western Asia around 2000 BCE and were the first to base their power on iron processing. Their civilization peaked around 1500 BCE.

Homo habilis hominid who walked upright and lived around 2 million years ago; first hominid species to be found in association with manufactured tools.

Homo sapiens sapiens modern man; developed around 100,000 years ago; displaced Neanderthals around 30,000 years ago.

Horus Egyptian sun god and son of Osiris; represented as a falcon.

Hyksos Asiatic people who settled in Egypt during the 17th century BCE. They later ruled the kingdom.

Iberians non-Celtic Iron Age people of Spain and southern France. The high point of their culture was from the fifth to the third century BCE.

ice ages climatic episodes characterized by a great drop in temperature, the expansion of ice caps at regions of higher latitude, and changes in flora and fauna.

Inanna Sumerian fertility goddess; daughter of Anu (the god of heaven and ruler of the gods).

Indo-European languages common family of European and Asiatic (Indian) languages.

iron metallic element that can be made into tools, weapons, and ornaments. Iron was being processed in western Asia by 3000 BCE.

Iron Age period during which major tools and weapons were made of iron; followed the Bronze Age. The Hittites formed the first Iron Age culture around 1700 BCE.

Ishtar Semitic war goddess who merged with Inanna and became the goddess of love and fertility.

Kush kingdom of southern Egypt; part of modern Sudan. In the Late period, the Kushites ruled Egypt.

Lagash Sumerian city-state that constituted a dominant empire in Mesopotamia in the 22nd century BCE.

La Tène culture Celtic Iron Age culture (c. 500–40 BCE); named for the site in Switzerland at which its artifacts were first discovered.

Late period era, from around 671 BCE, when Egypt was ruled by a

succession of foreign powers: the Kushites, the Assyrians, the Persians, and finally, in 332 BCE, the Greeks under Alexander the Great.

Linearbandceramik culture Neolithic culture of northern and central Europe dating from around 5000 BCE; recognized by its pottery decorations of distinct wavy or zigzag patterns.

lugal political leader in the Sumerian city-states.

Medes Indo-European people who entered northeastern Iran around the 17th century BCE.

megaliths large prehistoric stone monuments.

Memphis city in Lower (northern) Egypt; residence of the pharaohs during the Old Kingdom and during the time of the Ramesside kings.

menhirs pillarlike stone monuments or megaliths that may have marked sacrificial sites.

Mesopotamia area in western Asia between the Euphrates and Tigris rivers; location of several of the world's first great civilizations, including that of Sumer.

Middle Kingdom period of Egyptian history, from around 2150 to 1550 BCE, during which unity was restored by the Theban kings.

Mitanni Hurrian kingdom that flourished in northern Mesopotamia from around 1500 to 1350 BCE.

mummification method of preserving human remains by embalming.

Neanderthal archaic branch of *Homo sapiens* classified today as *Homo sapiens Neanderthalensis*; lived between 75,000 and 30,000 years ago in Europe and Asia.

Neolithic period era that lasted from around 8000 to 2000 BCE; characterized by a shift from hunting and gathering to domestication of plants and animals; also known as the New Stone Age.

New Kingdom period of Egyptian history that lasted from around 1550 to 1075 BCE.

Nile world's longest river; flows north from central Africa into Egypt. All of the great cities of ancient Egypt grew up on its banks.

Nineveh city of the ancient Assyrian Empire; situated on the east bank of the Tigris River opposite modern Mosul (Iraq).

Nubia region in Africa, extending approximately from the Nile River Valley to the shores of the Red Sea, southward to Khartoum, and westward to the Libyan Desert.

obsidian natural glass of volcanic origin that is formed by the rapid cooling of lava.

Old Kingdom period of Egyptian history that lasted from around 2650 to 2150 BCE.

Osiris ancient Egyptian god of death and the underworld.

Paleolithic period era that lasted from around 1.6 million years ago to 10,000 BCE; also known as the Old Stone Age.

pharaoh Egyptian king, who also acted as legislator, military general, and religious leader. Later, he was considered the son of Re.

Phoenicia ancient region roughly corresponding to modern Lebanon. Its inhabitants, the Phoenicians, were merchants, traders, and colonizers of the Mediterranean region in the first millennium BCE.

Pleistocene epoch period between 1.8 million and 10,000 years ago during which the ice ages occurred.

prehistory period of human history before the development of writing; knowledge of this time is based on archaeological sources and scientific dating methods.

pyramid Egyptian royal tomb with triangular sides and a square base. Pyramid construction reached its height between around 2600 and 2400 BCE.

Re Egyptian sun god. The pharaoh was considered his son and ascended to his heavenly empire after death.

relief figurative sculpture that projects from a supporting background, which is usually a plane surface.

Scythians nomadic people who migrated from central Asia to the northern coast of the Black Sea in the eighth and seventh centuries BCE.

Sea Peoples maritime warriors of uncertain origin who invaded Egypt and other coastal regions of the eastern Mediterranean Sea at the end of the Bronze Age.

Semites people residing in northern and southern Mesopotamia. They spoke a different language from the Sumerians and largely dwelt in rural areas. They founded the Akkadian Empire around 2335 BCE.

stele standing stone slab used in the ancient world either to mark the site of a grave or to commemorate a historic event.

Stone Age earliest period of human civilization, from around 2 million BCE to around 3500 BCE.

Sumerians people of Sumer, in Mesopotamia, the site of the earliest known civilization, which emerged around 3400 BCE.

Tigris great river of western Asia that flows from the mountains of eastern Turkey to the Persian Gulf. Its lower reaches form the eastern edge of Mesopotamia.

tumuli Neolithic burial mounds.

tundra expanse of flat or gently undulating treeless land in cold regions; composed mainly of bare rock or ground covered with moss and lichen.

Unetician culture Bronze Age culture of central Europe.

Ur Sumerian city-state that constituted a centralized empire in Mesopotamia from around 2100 to 2000 BCE.

Urnfield culture late Bronze Age culture found throughout central Europe between around 1200 and 1000 BCE; named for the way in which the ashes of the deceased were buried in urns.

Uruk Sumerian city-state in Mesopotamia to the northwest of Ur. The ancient site was first excavated in 1928 CE.

Valley of the Kings area on the western bank of the Nile River opposite Thebes. New Kingdom pharaohs were buried there.

vizier high Egyptian administrative official; usually a close relative of the pharaoh.

ziggurat pyramidal, stepped temple towers built from brick in Mesopotamia between around 2200 and 500 BCE.

MAJOR HISTORICAL FIGURES

Ahmose pharaoh from 1550 to 1525 BCE; drove the Hyksos from Egypt and conquered their territory in western Asia; subjugated the Kushites.

Akhenaton pharaoh from 1353 to 1335 BCE; introduced the monotheistic cult of Aton to Egypt; built a new royal residence at Akhetaton.

Amenemhet I pharaoh from 1991 to 1962 BCE; restored unity to Egypt after the civil war that followed the death of his predecessor.

Amenemhet III pharaoh from 1843 to 1797 BCE; brought Egypt's Middle Kingdom to a peak of prosperity.

Carter, Howard (1874–1939 CE) British archaeologist who, in 1922 CE, discovered the tomb of the Egyptian king Tutankhamen.

Djoser pharaoh from around 2630 to 2611 BCE; presided over Egypt's first cultural flowering. The Step Pyramid was built for him at Saqqara.

Gudea ruler (*ensi*) of Lagash from around 2141 to 2122 BCE; famous for overseeing the construction of a temple to the god Ningirsu and the building hymn celebrating his accomplishment.

Hammurabi king of Babylon from around 1792 to 1750 BCE; defeated the kings of Larsa and Assur and conquered Mari; drew up a legal code and abolished the deification of kings.

Hatshepsut only female pharaoh; ruled Egypt from around 1473 to 1458 BCE.

Herod Roman-appointed king of Judaea from 37 to 4 BCE. Jesus was born in Bethlehem during Herod's reign.

Imhotep Egyptian architect who lived in the 27th century BCE; built the Step Pyramid at Saqqara on the orders of the pharaoh Djoser. Imhotep was deified after his death.

Kamose pharaoh from 1554 to 1550 BCE; tried to expel the Hyksos from the north and thwarted their attempts to form an alliance with the Kushites.

Lugalzaggisi king of the Sumerian city-state of Umma in the 24th century BCE.

Manetho priest who drew up a history of Egypt in the third century BCE and divided the pharaohs into dynasties.

Mentuhotep II pharaoh from 2061 to 2010 BCE; reunified Egypt around 2047 BCE by defeating his rivals and ushered in the period known as the Middle Kingdom.

Naram-Sin king of the Akkadian Empire from around 2254 to 2218 BCE; suppressed a rebellion by the Sumerian cities and conquered the areas surrounding Mesopotamia.

Nebuchadnezzar II king of Neo-Babylonian Empire from 605 to 562 BCE; conquered Syria, Phoenicia, and Judaea; built Babylon into an impressive capital.

Oppert, Jules (1825–1905 CE) French pioneer of research into the Sumerian language.

Sargon the Great founded the Akkadian Empire around 2335 BCE; based his power on the state monopoly of raw materials.

Sesostris I pharaoh from 1962 to 1926 BCE during the Middle Kingdom period; brought Egypt to the height of its prosperity.

Sesostris III pharaoh from 1878 to 1843 BCE; ended the power and independence of the local administrators; established a centralized system of royal supervisors; expanded Egyptian territory into Palestine.

Thomsen, Christian (1788–1865 CE) Danish archaeologist who devised the division of early human history into three ages: the Stone Age, the Bronze Age, and the Iron Age.

Tutankhamen pharaoh from around 1332 to 1323 BCE; left the royal residence at Akhetaton and resumed the cult of deities to reduce the chaos and dissatisfaction that had been created by Akhenaton. Tutankhamen's grave was left untouched and contained precious funerary treasures.

Woolley, Leonard (1880–1960 CE) British archaeologist who excavated the ancient city of Ur in Mesopotamia; also worked on the excavation of the Hittite city of Carchemish.

RESOURCES FOR FURTHER STUDY

BOOKS

Adams, Robert McC. *The Evolution of Urban Society: Early Mesopotamia and Prehispanic Mexico.* Chicago, IL, 1966.

Anthony, David W. *The Horse, the Wheel, and Language: How Bronze-Age Riders from the Eurasian Steppes Shaped the Modern World.* Princeton, NJ, 2007.

Bahn, Paul (ed.). *The Atlas of World Archaeology.* New York, 2000.

Bahn, Paul. *Journey Through the Ice Age.* Berkeley, CA, 1997.

Baines, John, and Jaromir Malek. *Atlas of Ancient Egypt.* New York, 2002.

Bancroft Hunt, Norman. *Historical Atlas of Ancient Mesopotamia.* New York, 2004.

Brier, Bob. *Egyptian Mummies: Unraveling the Secrets of an Ancient Art.* New York, 1994.

Burke, John, and Kaj Halberg. *Seed of Knowledge, Stone of Plenty: Understanding the Lost Technology of the Megalith Builders.* San Francisco, CA, 2005.

Chadwick, Robert. *First Civilizations: Ancient Mesopotamia and Ancient Egypt.* Oakville, CT, 2005.

Clayton, Peter A. *Chronicle of the Pharaohs: The Reign-by-Reign Record of the Rulers and Dynasties of Ancient Egypt.* New York, 1994.

Cotterell, Arthur (ed.). *The Penguin Encyclopedia of Ancient Civilizations.* New York, 1988.

Curtis, Gregory. *The Cave Painters: Probing the Mysteries of the World's First Artists.* New York, 2007.

Dorling Kindersley Publishing. *Early Humans.* New York, 2005.

Hawass, Zahi A. *The Golden Age of Tutankhamun: Divine Might and Splendor in the New Kingdom.* New York, 2004.

Haywood, John. *Ancient Civilizations of the Near East and Mediterranean.* Armonk, NY, 1997.

Hodder, Ian. *Theory and Practice in Archaeology.* New York, 1992.

Hoffman, Michael A. *Egypt before the Pharaohs.* New York, 1979.

Honan, Linda. *Spend the Day in Ancient Egypt: Projects and Activities that Bring the Past to Life.* New York, 1999.

Hynes, Margaret. *The Best Book of Early People.* New York, 2003.

James, T.G.H. *A Short History of Ancient Egypt: From Predynastic to Roman Times.* Baltimore, MD, 1998.

Kramer, Samuel Noah. *The Sumerians: Their History, Culture, and Character.* Chicago, IL, 1963.

Langley, Andrew. *Ancient Egypt.* Chicago, IL, 2005.

Leakey, Richard E. *The Origin of Humankind.* New York, 1994.

Liverani, Mario (edited and translated by Zainab Bahrani and Marc Van De Mieroop). *Uruk: The First City.* Oakville, Ontario, Canada, 2006.

Macaulay, David. *Pyramid.* Boston, MA, 1975.

Maisels, Charles. *The Emergence of Civilization.* London, England, 1990.

————. *The Near East: Archaeology in the Cradle of Civilization.* London, England, 1993.

McIntosh, Jane. *Ancient Mesopotamia: New Perspectives.* Santa Barbara, CA, 2005.

Megaw, M. Ruth, and Vincent Megaw. *Celtic Art: From Its Beginnings to the Book of Kells.* New York, 2001.

Mitchell, Stephen. *Gilgamesh: A New English Version.* New York, 2004.

Mithen, Steven J. *After the Ice: A Global Human History, 20,000–5000 BC.* Cambridge, MA, 2004.

Moorey, P.R.S. *Ancient Mesopotamian Materials and Industries: The Archaeological Evidence.* Oxford, England, 1994.

Oakes, Lorna, and Philip Steele. *Everyday Life in Ancient Egypt and Mesopotamia*. London, England, 2006.

Oates, David, and Joan Oates. *The Rise of Civilization*. Oxford, England, 1976.

Postgate, Nicholas. *Early Mesopotamia: Society and Economy at the Dawn of History*. London, England, 1992.

Redman, Charles. *The Rise of Civilization*. San Francisco, CA, 1978.

Reeves, C.N., and Richard H. Wilkinson. *The Complete Valley of the Kings: Tombs and Treasures of Egypt's Greatest Pharaohs*. New York, 1996.

Roaf, Michael. *Cultural Atlas of Mesopotamia and the Ancient Near East*. New York, 1990.

Robins, Gay. *Women in Ancient Egypt*. Cambridge, MA, 1993.

Romer, John. *The Great Pyramid: Ancient Egypt Revisited*. New York, 2007.

Ross, Stewart. *Ancient Egypt*. Milwaukee, WI, 2005.

Rudgley, Richard. *The Lost Civilizations of the Stone Age*. New York, 1999.

Saggs, H.W.F. *Babylonians*. London, England, 2000.

Scarre, Christopher, and Brian M. Fagan. *Ancient Civilizations*. Upper Saddle River, NJ, 2008.

Schomp, Virginia. *Ancient Mesopotamia: The Sumerians, Babylonians, and Assyrians*. New York, 2005.

Shanower, Eric. *Age of Bronze* (3 volumes). Orange, CA, 2001.

Shaw, Ina (ed.). *The Oxford History of Ancient Egypt*. New York, 2003.

Silverman, David P. (ed.). *Ancient Egypt*. New York, 2003.

Steward, Julian (ed.). *Irrigation Civilizations: A Comparative Study*. Washington, DC, 1955.

Time-Life Books. *Ancient Civilizations, 3000 BC–AD 500*. Alexandria, VA, 1998.

———. *Egypt: Land of the Pharaohs*. Alexandria, VA, 1992.

———. *Sumer: Cities of Eden*. Alexandria, VA, 1993.

Vanstiphout, H.L.J. *Epics of Sumerian Kings: The Matter of Aratta*. Boston, MA, 2004.

Wilkinson, Toby (ed.). *The Egyptian World*. New York, 2007.

Wiseman, D.J. *Nebuchadrezzar and Babylon*. New York, 1985.

Wittfogel, Karl A. *Oriental Despotism: A Comparative Study of Total Power*. New Haven, CT, 1957.

Zettler, Richard L., and Lee Horne (eds.). *Treasures from the Royal Tombs of Ur*. Philadelphia, PA, 1998.

WEB SITES

American Museum of Natural History
A wealth of information on anthropology and paleontology
http://www.amnh.org

Ancient Egypt
Web site that is dedicated to ancient Egypt and Egyptology
http://www.ancientegypt.co.uk

Ancient Egyptian Gods
Web site that provides facts about 12 of the most important Egyptian gods
http://www.bbc.co.uk/history/ancient/egyptians/gods_gallery_01.shtml

Ancient Sumeria
Aspects of life in ancient Sumeria
http://history-world.org/sumeria.htm

Celtic Art
Descriptions and illustrations of a wide range of ancient Celtic art forms, from body decoration to megaliths
http://www.freeceltic.com

Code of Hammurabi
Online version of the full text, translated by L.W. King and edited by Richard Hooker
http://www.wsu.edu/~dee/MESO/CODE.HTM

Egypt's Golden Empire
Web site that accompanies the PBS series
http://www.pbs.org/empires/egypt

Funnel-Beaker Culture
Overview with suggestions for further study
http://www.comp-archaeology.org/TRB.htm

Great Ice Age
Downloadable text containing a summary of information
about the last ice age
http://pubs.usgs.gov/gip/ice_age

Iraq National Museum
Includes photographs of many Mesopotamian artifacts held
by the museum
http://www.baghdadmuseum.org/home.php

Iron Age in Western Europe
Web site that includes photographs of La Tène artifacts
http://www.hp.uab.edu/image_archive/uj/ujk.html

Mesopotamia
Web site that features separate sections on Assyria,
Babylonia, and Sumer
http://www.mesopotamia.co.uk

Mesopotamian Cultures
Web site that features information on various
Mesopotamian cultures
http://www.wsu.edu/~dee/MESO/MESO.HTM

Oriental Institute of the University of Chicago
Photographs of archaeological sites at Uruk and links to
other places and topics of related interest
http://oi.uchicago.edu/gallery/asp_meso_uruk

Pharaohs
Web site that provides a full list of ancient rulers and
related information
http://www.touregypt.net/kings.htm

Pyramids
Web site that contains facts about Egypt's pyramids and the
pharaohs buried inside them
http://www.nationalgeographic.com/pyramids/pyramids.html

Secrets of the Pharaohs
Web site that accompanies a PBS series investigating
some of the mysteries of ancient Egypt; includes links
to maps, resources, and time lines
http://www.pbs.org/wnet/pharaohs/about.html

Skara Brae
Photographs of the Stone Age settlement
*http://www.bbc.co.uk/history/ancient/british_prehistory/skara_
brae_gallery.shtml*

Stone Age Institute
Web site that highlights the latest anthropological and
archaeological research into the period
http://www.stoneageinstitute.org

Tutankhamen's Tomb
Guide to the treasures of the pharaoh's tomb
http://www.nationalgeographic.com/egypt

Ur
Illustrated history
*http://www.mnsu.edu/emuseum/archaeology/sites/middle_east/
ur.html*

Venus of Willendorf
Web site about the famous prehistoric figurine
http://witcombe.sbc.edu/willendorf/willendorfdiscovery.html

INDEX